The Retirement Epidemic

The Retirement Epidemic

How to Finally Get the Cure to the Infected Status Quo

AMIR HEYDARI

The Retirement Epidemic

© 2018 Amir Heydari

All rights reserved. No portion of this book may be reproduced, stored in a retrieval system, or transmitted in any form or by any means-electronica, mechanical, photocopy, recording, scanning, or other, except for brief quotations in critical reviews or articles, without the prior written permission of the publisher.

ISBN: 978-1-7325893-9-1

Printed in the United States of America Year of First Printing: 2018

Cover Design by: Ken Wilcox

Disclaimer

While great efforts have been taken to provide accurate and current information regarding the covered material, neither the Heydari Wealth Group nor Amir Heydari are responsible for any errors or omissions, or for the results obtained from the use of this information.

The title, "The Retirement Epidemic," is a marketing concept and does not guarantee or imply that you will become wealthy. The act of purchasing any book, course, or financial product holds no such guarantees.

The ideas, suggestions, general principles, and conclusions presented here are subject to local, state and federal laws and regulations, and revisions of same, and are intended for informational purposes only. All information in this report is provided "as is" with no guarantee of completeness, accuracy, or timeliness regarding the results obtained from the use of this information and without warranty of any kind, express or implied, including, but not limited to, warranties of performance, merchantability, and fitness for a particular purpose. Your use of this information is at your own risk.

You assume full responsibility and risk of loss resulting from the use of this information. Amir Heydari and the Heydari Wealth Group is not liable for any direct, special, indirect, incidental, consequential, or punitive damages or any other damages whatsoever, whether in an action based upon a statute, contract, tort (including, but not limited to negligence), or otherwise, relating to the use of this information.

In no event will Amir Heydari, the Heydari Wealth Group, or their related partnerships or corporations, or the partners, agents, or employees of Amir Heydari the Heydari Wealth Group be liable to you or anyone else for any decision made or action taken in reliance on the information in this book or for any consequential, special, or similar damages, even if advised of the possibility of such damages.

Neither Amir Heydari nor the Heydari Wealth Group are engaged in rendering legal, accounting, or other professional services. If accounting, financial, legal, or tax advice is required, the services of a competent professional should be sought.

Facts and information in this book are believed to be accurate at the time of publication and may become outdated by marketplace changes or conditions, new

Disclaimer

or revised laws, or other circumstances. All figures and examples in this report are based on rates and assumptions no later in time than August 2018. Rates and assumptions are not guaranteed and may be subject to change. As in all assumptions and examples, individual results may vary based on a wide range of factors unique to each person's situation. All data provided in this book are to be used for informational purposes only. Any slights against individuals, companies, or organizations are unintentional.

TABLE OF CONTENTS

Disclaimer 5

Chapter One:
Is the American Dream Still Alive? 13

Chapter Two:
America's Incurable Disease 20

Chapter Three:
Your Government Plan Isn't What It Seems 36

Chapter Four:
How Much Does Market Loss Really Cost? 52

Chapter Five:
Is This Your Biggest Retirement Risk? 70

Chapter Six:
Inflation, Interest Rates, and Your Erroneous Nest Egg 87

Chapter Seven:
Is There A Perfect Investment? 102

Chapter Eight:
What Do You Know About These Popular Private Wealth Strategies? 113

Chapter Nine:
Curing the Retirement Income Gap 128

Chapter Ten:
The Power of the Index 145

Chapter Eleven:
Do You Blindly Follow The Status Quo? 161

Chapter Twelve:
How to Grow Your Money Through the Power of Indexed Arbitrage 175

Chapter Thirteen:
Leveraged Wealth Arbitrage 185

CALL TO ACTION 201

ACKNOWLEDGEMENTS 203

End Notes 205

The Retirement Epidemic

How to Finally Get the Cure to the Broken Status Quo

AMIR HEYDARI

Chapter One:

Is the American Dream Still Alive?

I have a story to tell...
   One being twisted by the media.
   Told incorrectly by Washington politicians.
   And even forgotten by most.
   It's about this blessed country called America.
   Where the dream of building a different life for yourself exists for each and every person...regardless of your background, nationality, gender, or race.
   It is not easy for most. Yet it is possible, with the right vision and focus.
   If you truly desire it.
   This is a story that when I look back, shocks me, even gives me goose bumps, thinking about where I started... to where I am now.

I moved to America in the summer of 1997.

I wasn't alone. I moved here with my mother, brother, and sister.

We weren't native English speakers, and I remember that the language barrier was a massive issue. In those days, I was pretty shy.

I didn't know a word of English.

For months, I walked the halls of my high school, deaf to the conversations in English that were happening all around me. I sat in my classrooms, completely lost, unable to comprehend a word of what the teacher was saying.

It was tough!

When I came here, I not only couldn't speak the language, I didn't know the cultural differences. It took me well over a year to acclimate to the culture, the customs, and the language.

At first, I begrudged having to work so hard, but now I realize what a blessing it was. It made me who I am today and gave me the skills I needed to achieve so much because I had to work harder, study longer, and be better than those around me.

Today I am very grateful for that experience.

Through hard work, endurance, and a vision of what you want your life to be comes the bliss and joy of achieving your dreams and goals...and hopefully sharing it with those you love.

How Visiting My Friend's Parents Changed My Life

After high school, I went to college. Cal State Los Angeles. I pursued a degree in finance because I wanted to work in the stock market. In my favorite class, Finance 304, we traded stocks but weren't allowed to use real money because we were still in school. But It felt just like real money and it was exciting to see a huge, quick gain on my trades. Most of my trades were in the green. I had some bad trades, but overall, out of all my classmates, I was the #1 trader by a large margin.

Trading seemed to fit me well, but during my college years, I traded with money that wasn't real. There is no emotional attachment to money that isn't real because it doesn't belong to anyone, neither me nor my clients.

I kept throwing money at the market because I had nothing to lose.

Things went extremely well during that time. I felt like the world was my oyster. I knew trading was what I wanted to do and working on Wall Street was within my grasp.

Then an experience at a friend's house shocked my reality.

Right before graduating, I went with a friend to visit his parents and right away, I could see they were very worried.

They knew I was studying finance, so my friend's mother gathered up a bunch of statements from their investments and handed them to me.

"Can you take a look and tell me what you think?" she asked, her hands trembling slightly as she held out the stack of paper.

Looking closer I could see that they had $7 million in an account that was divided between three siblings. The money was invested in stocks, mutual funds, and bonds.

As I continued looking through the stack of statements, I could see that their account had gone from $7 million to $4 million in only six months! My friend's parents had been receiving statements but hadn't really looked at any of them. They weren't very savvy when it came to their investments.

These people lost almost half of their money in six months and I had never seen anything like it.

When I explained the situation to my friend's parents, his father looked at me and said, "Why is this happening?"

I looked at him and couldn't give him a solid response. They were a little bit older and the money was meant to support them in retirement. What were they going to do?

My Friend's Parents Lost Real Money

Seeing how their account was affected over time changed the way I thought about money and caused me to dive deeper in why this happened to my best friend. Here I was, trading *fake* money, while my friend's parents had lost *real* money…and a lot of it.

So, I started doing some research and soon realized that the market wasn't all that great. My class hadn't taught me how often market crashes happen and just how devastating they can be.

There was no doubt that their retirement would be negatively affected by the loss, by <u>real loss</u>.

I thought, *Do I really want to get into the stock market now?*

I was so in love with stocks. I was trading fake money and making big (albeit not real) bucks. It was fun. But what happened to my friend's parents, that moment in the kitchen when I looked through that stack of statements, had a big impact on what I decided to do later on. It pushed me away from the market.

If this was my money, how would I feel?

Can I Use My Finance Degree to Help People?

The experience with my friend's parents had been haunting. It happened in 2008, the same year I graduated college. I knew I didn't want to get into the stock market anymore but wasn't sure exactly what to do with my finance degree.

I thought back to my friend's parents. The look on their faces when they realized they had lost almost half of their retirement savings was devastating. I never wanted anyone to experience anything like that, ever again.

What if I can use my degree to *help* people?

What if I can educate people so they don't make the same mistakes as my friend's parents?

I decided to go into business for myself, so I could focus on helping people.

I knew it would be tough, but fortunately the decision to go for it came easily to me because I had been here before. Nothing could be harder than moving to a new country in the middle of high school, right?

Those years were very tough for me and harder than I thought they would be. I started with nothing, but through trial and error, gained invaluable experience and developed critical skills.

Armed with those skills and my own personal experiences as an immigrant trying to make a name for himself in America, I have cultivated a unique expertise that has allowed me to grow and protect my own wealth, and the wealth of my clients, by leaps and bounds.

I want to safeguard the money my clients worked so hard to earn. I want it to be secure and safe, so one day when they need it, it's going to be there for them.

Most of the people I talk to today don't have a very good idea of the different solutions out there. They don't know about all their options. Most Americans have 401(k)s because most of the time its included in the employees benefits and it's the only retirement vehicle they know.

There are many different strategies and tools out there and some are a lot better than others.

Which one is best for you?

Well, that really depends on what you want.

I want to show you some of your options, so you can make financial decisions to keep your money safe.

That's why I'm writing this book. I don't want what happened to my friend's parents to happen to anyone… and with the right education and the right information, it really doesn't have to.

When I moved to America, I didn't speak the language or know the customs, but now I am financially secure, and my retirement is protected.

Is the American Dream still alive?

With hard work, commitment, and a little education, I believe that it most certainly is still alive.

Chapter Two:
America's Incurable Disease

When I was 25, my entire life changed. I was young, I was fit, and I was fresh out of college, looking for a job.

One day, I decided to take a break from my job search and go to the doctor for my annual physical. It was my first physical in a couple of years and I was due for some blood work.

On my way there I thought, *I'm 25 years old and I'm invincible! I'm not going to have any issues. I'm healthy and I work out.*

When I arrived, I checked in, and a short 45-minutes later, I left. Easy, right?

A few days later, that feeling of ease started to disappear. There were concerns about my bloodwork and X-rays, and I needed to come back in for more testing.

On Sept 25, 2008, I waited in the doctor's office.

He must be wrong. I don't feel sick.

I tried to convince myself this wasn't happening to me, but my hands were sweating as I looked around the waiting room, hoping to spot something that would take my mind off the nightmare.

Just then, the door leading to the examinations rooms opened and a nurse stepped out.

"Mr. Heydari, the doctor will see you now."

As I stood up from my chair and headed toward her, I could feel the fear growing inside my stomach. It was a nervous, tight energy that shook my very core.

I followed her in and heard the door slam behind me. It was surreal, ominous, and eerie, like in a movie. It felt like I was never going to leave the facility.

It felt like ages had passed by the time the doctor finally stepped into the examination room to talk to me.

"There isn't an easy way to say this, but you have cancer."

The news hit me like a ton of bricks.

I was 25 years old and I had cancer.

Is this happening?

Am I dreaming?

I'm only 25!

Before I knew it, I was on the operating table. It was a success, but I still wasn't done. I still had three weeks of radiation, which was probably the worst part.

Thankfully, I made it through radiation and today I'm still cancer-free.

America's Retirement Epidemic

America is suffering from its own unique cancer, a sneaky disease that has been growing and festering for decades.

I'm talking about America's Retirement Income Crisis, a plague aimed at ruining the hopes and dreams of retirees across the country.

Is there a retirement income crisis?

I believe wholeheartedly that there is. People aren't saving enough for retirement. It's an epidemic.

Retirement Savings Have Stagnated in the New Millennium
Mean retirement account savings of families by age, 1989-2013 (2013 dollars)

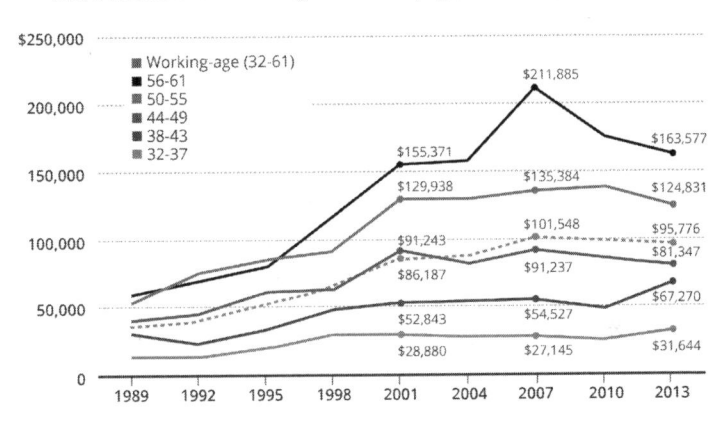

Year	Working-age (32-61)	56-61	50-55	44-49	38-43	32-37
2001	$91,243	$155,371	$129,938	$91,243	$86,187	$52,843 / $28,880
2007		$211,885	$135,384	$101,548	$91,237	$54,527 / $27,145
2013		$163,577	$124,831	$95,776	$81,347	$67,270 / $31,644

Note: Retirement account savings include 401(k)s, IRAs, and Keogh plans.
Source: EPI analysis of Survey of Consumer Finance data, 2013.

A 2016 Economic Policy Institute report revealed the extent of the disease's devastation. In 2013, the average American family between the ages of 56 and 61 had only $163,577 saved[1]. And that's the **mean**, the *average*. When we look at the **median**, the middle value, that number plummets. Suddenly we're looking at $17,000 in retirement savings...

Meaning more than half of Americans between the ages of 56 and 61 have less than $17,000 saved for retirement.

Most Families - Even Those Approaching Retirement - Have Little or No Retirement Savings

Mean retirement account savings of families by age, 1989-2013 (2013 dollars)

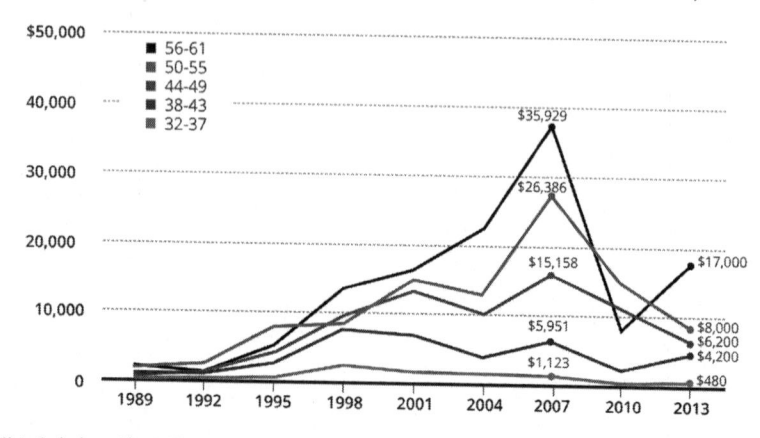

- 56-61
- 50-55
- 44-49
- 38-43
- 32-37

Key values shown: $35,929; $26,386; $15,158; $5,951; $1,123; $17,000; $8,000; $6,200; $4,200; $480

Note: Scale changed for visibility. Retirement account savings include 401(k)s, IRAs, and Keogh plans.
Source: EPI analysis of Survey of Consumer Finance data, 2013.

How long do you think that retirement savings is going to last?

We're All Living Longer

America's Retirement Income Crisis is an epidemic, an epidemic I believe began with the shift in the way America retires. In the next chapter, we'll get into that concept in more detail, but that shift began because people started living longer.

Just how much longer?

In 1900, the average life expectancy was 46.3 for men and 48.3 for women, and in 1950, those ages climbed to 65.6 and 71.1, respectively[2]. Today, the average life expectancy for men is 76.9 and 81.8 for women[3].

Life Expectancy 1900-2018		
	Male	Female
1900	46.3	48.3
1950	65.6	71.1
2018	76.9	81.8

In 2030, the World Health Organization predicts the average life expectancy for females living in countries like the U.S. will be 85[4].

A longer lifespan means a longer retirement. If the average retiree leaves the workforce at age 65, and lives until 85, he or she will have to plan for 20 years of retirement!

Let's break this down into a practical example.

Earlier, I stated that the average American family, between the ages of 56 and 61, has $163,577 saved for retirement. In order to make that last for 20 years, our average American family can only give itself $8,179 a year, or $682 a month in retirement.

Is that enough?

Savings	$163,577
Retirement	20 years
Annual Income	$8,179
Monthly Income	$682

I don't know anyone who can survive on $682 a month. Do you?

The sad truth is that many of America's retirees will find themselves with a lack of sufficient income in retirement.

The Federal Reserve's Survey of Consumer Finances (SCF) shows households with retirement accounts only have a third of the funds needed to maintain their standard of living. Over 74% of people over age 40 are behind schedule for retirement[5], and according to the Center for Retirement Research at Boston College, <u>52% of working Americans will be unable to maintain their standard of living in retirement</u>[6].

What does that mean?

Lifestyle reduction. A series of trade-offs at best, and major sacrifices at worst. You might have to trade that international vacation for something domestic...or skip it all together.

But for many, it could be much worse than that. It's one thing to change vacation plans or accept a slightly reduced standard of living and be forced to downsize to an apartment when you'd rather remain in the family home.

It's quite another to choose between keeping the lights on or buying medicine or food.

For many Americans, that's the reality they will likely face.

And they know it.

The most recent Gallup survey found that 54% of Americans are worried about retirement[7].

So, what's the problem? Why is this happening?

The Retirement Epidemic's 6 Biggest Symptoms

America's biggest fear is running out of money[8], yet the majority of us aren't saving enough.

Why?

Well, every disease has symptoms, right? Let's take a look at the biggest six.

Symptom #1: Dependability on Government Plans

Many of us are relying on social security and the money in our **qualified plan** (401(k), 403(b), IRA) to support us in retirement.

The problem is that if you rely on these plans, you're relying on the government to support you in retirement.

Social security in the U.S. is a government system designed to provide financial assistance to those who can no longer work. While you're employed, you pay into the system via taxes and receive benefits when it's time for you to retire[9]. The amount you receive in retirement is directly related to the amount of social security taxes you contributed throughout your working life.

Do you know what that equates to in retirement?

Currently, the average retiree receiving social security benefits sees $1,368/month or $16,416/year[10]. That's only a thousand dollars above the individual poverty level ($15,060 in 2017[11]).

For a small percentage of the population, $1,368 a month might be enough, but for many of us, it doesn't even come close!

Do you think your 401(k), 403(b), and/or IRA will cover the difference?

Think again.

These plans are all tied to the United States tax system. Pre-tax doesn't mean tax-free (we'll get into that more later), meaning you will have to pay taxes when you take that money out.

Do you know what the tax rate is going to be in the future?

No one does!

But at the rate our current government deficit is increasing, what do you think is likely to happen?

Ultimately, the government controls the tax code. Do you really want your retirement tied to the government and the tax code?

Symptom #2: Market Losses & Opportunity Costs

Wall Street wants you to believe that if you stay in the market long enough, regardless of the losses, your money will always come back. If you keep your money invested for 20 years, you might see negative returns for a few years, but it's all going to come back eventually.

Right?

It comes back because you continue to contribute to that account, not because money magically reappears. If you have a 401(k) account, and you keep funding it, it's going to come back.

The market is going to rebound, that's going to help, but the *new* money that you put into the account is going to make the account come back, not the lost money. That money is gone forever.

Your inability to reinvest that lost money is an **opportunity cost**. If you drop your wallet and lose $20, you can no longer earn interest on that $20 because you no longer have the opportunity to invest that money and earn interest on it.

Market losses are directly related to opportunity costs because every dollar lost represents a potential compound loss. It's those losses that can negatively impact our retirement savings because oftentimes they are costlier than the original lost amount.

Later, we'll go into more detail about this concept, but for now, let me give you a brief example.

If a 45-year-old male loses $50,000 in the market, his opportunity cost is $200,000 over 20 years, and just over $850,000 in his lifetime (based on average life expectancy).

Meaning, if he were to keep that $50,000 in a safe account, and grow it at an average of 7%, it would grow to $200,000 in 20 years and $850,000 in his lifetime. His real loss is much bigger than the original $50,000. That's why losses in the market are so devastating.

Original Investment	$50,000
Average Growth	7%
Value After 20 Years	$200,000
Value After 30 Years	$850,000

Can your retirement savings afford to lose $850,000 over its lifetime?

Symptom #3: Future Taxes

Another symptom is that many Americans aren't accounting for future taxes.

Most of us save for retirement in 401(k)s, 403(b)s, and other tax-deferred, qualified accounts. These accounts allow us to make pre-tax deposits, potentially lowering our annual taxable income. The idea is that these accounts are supposed to help us save money on taxes *now*.

But what about tomorrow?

Pre-tax accounts allow you to save money on taxes now, but tomorrow, when it's time to take that money out, you have to pay. If I contribute $15,000 to my 401(k) this year, I will be expected to pay taxes on that $15,000 and any growth when I retire and withdraw it.

Do you think taxes will be more or less in the future?

Every day, we are taxed on everything. We are taxed on the gas in our cars, the groceries we buy, and the houses we live in. There's property tax, income tax, and sales tax. You're even taxed when you die.

Every year, the Fed adds another tax. Soon they're going to tax us for breathing air, right?

Taxes are scary enough when we know what to expect...but how do we plan for something unknown?

Ed Slott is one of the most well-known CPAs in the country. He states that taxes are the single biggest retirement risk because they are undetermined[12]. Nobody knows what the tax rate is going to be in the future.

"Do you know what your income tax rate is going to be when you retire?"

"I hope it's going to be lower."

What happens if they aren't? What if taxes are *higher*?

And if they are higher, what does that do to your retirement savings? How much money will you lose?

More on this later, but most people don't know that the highest marginal tax rate was almost 94% and the lowest was 23%[13]. Today, the high is 35% and the low is only 10%.

Symptom #4: Inflation

Inflation is sneaky. We all know it exists, yet we tend to forget about it when planning for retirement.

But if we don't plan for it, we could end up suffering in retirement.

For example, let's say today you need $100,000 in annual income to support your lifestyle.

Do you think $100,000 will be enough 20 years from now? How about 30 years?

Most likely not.

Because we all know that over time, as the price of goods goes up, the value of our money goes down.

Symptom #5: Interest Rates:

Did you know that as of 2017, Americans have amassed over $8.74 trillion in mortgages[14]?

That's a lot of interest.

Every day, millions of Americans are losing millions of dollars to interest rates. In a world consumed with instant gratification, people have been trained to buy now and pay later. We spend money we don't have on things we can't afford, then we stress out because no matter how hard we try, we can't get out of debt. We can't get ahead.

Interest rates are Symptom #5, because they are avoidable, and money paid in interest could instead be turned into retirement savings.

Think about how much more you would have saved for retirement if you didn't have to pay interest.

Symptom #6: Your Erroneous Nest Egg

Do you have a "nest egg"? Do you have a stock-pile of money sitting in an account somewhere?

I talk to a lot of people who have a large "nest egg" or are looking to build one. Some of them even like to brag about the size of their nest egg.

It's good to have a nice nest egg, but when it comes to retirement planning, it's more important to look at cash flow because your nest egg, as big as it looks, still might not be enough.

That's why the erroneous nest egg is Symptom #6. People pick a number, save up until they reach it, and think they're done planning for retirement.

What is that million-dollar nest egg going to do for you if you have to pay 30% in taxes?

Would you rather have a $2 million "nest egg" in retirement or have a secured income of $70,000 a year for the rest of your life?

> ### 3 Types of Cash Flow
>
> Instead of focusing on your nest egg, you should be focusing on cash flow.
>
> There are three different types of cash flow:
>
> **#1) Passive Cash Flow** is regular, consistent income that requires little to no effort to maintain.
>
> **#2) Guaranteed Cash Flow** is money that you will receive for the rest of your life, no matter how long you live.
>
> **#3) Tax-Free Cash Flow** is money that isn't subjected to taxes.

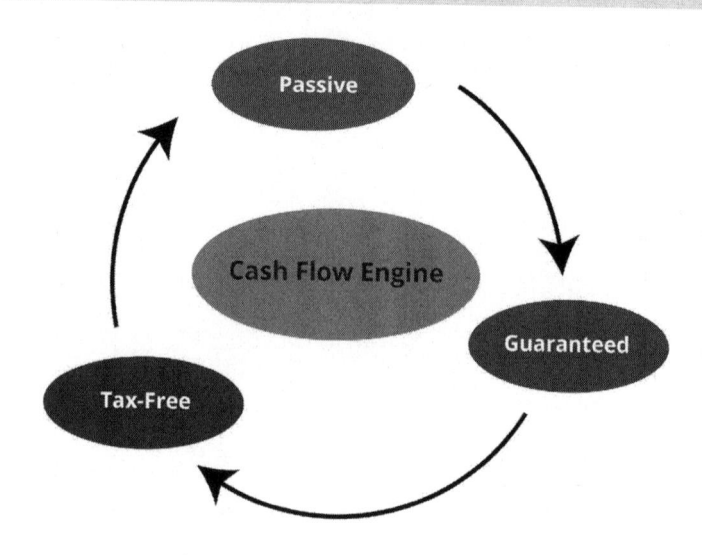

The Light at the End of the Tunnel

The Retirement Income Crisis is a cancerous epidemic that is infecting generations of retirees.

Too many of us are relying on social security, losing millions to market losses, opportunity costs, and taxes. We are also vastly overestimating the fortitude of our nest eggs.

Regardless of the symptom, the spread of this infectious disease must be stopped.

The good news is that there is hope. There is a light at the end of this dark, cancer-ridden retirement tunnel.

Over the 9+ years I've been in business, through trial and error, I have discovered little known strategies that can help boost your savings and generate additional income, all without having to change your lifestyle.

With the right strategy and the right tools, I can help grow your wealth, cancer free.

Chapter Three:

Your Government Plan Isn't What It Seems

Have you heard the story of the *Emperor's New Clothes?*

Years ago, there was an Emperor who had a thing for clothes. He was very interested in fashion and spent all his extra cash on the newest styles.

He really didn't care about anything else. He didn't care to manage his soldiers, compliment his staff, or even rule his people. He only cared about how well he was dressed.

One day, two con artists came to town, posing as fashion designers. They spoke loudly of their uniquely fine fabrics, patterns, and designs.

They also told the people of the town that their fabric was exclusive; if you were a fool, or unfit for your position, the fabric would appear invisible.

Next, the two fashion designers set up a weave in town square and began to create beautiful fabrics from spun wool.

Except, they didn't weave any fabric, at all. They're con artists, remember? They only *pretended* to weave.

No one saw the fabric (because it didn't exist), but no one questioned it because they assumed the fabric was invisible. The commoners saw nothing and simply assumed they were foolish, and the public officials (arrogantly assuming they weren't foolish), didn't want to admit they couldn't see the fabric because it would mean they were unfit for office.

The Emperor was no exception. When he went to see the wondrous clothing the fashion designers had been creating in his town, he hid his dismay. He saw *nothing*, but of course, couldn't admit it. That would mean he was unfit to be Emperor!

So, he purchased the clothing and undressed. The con artists then pretended to put the garments on the Emperor, one article of clothing at a time. He then proceeded to walk outside the dressing room and greet the crowd that had gathered.

When he stepped out into the sunlight, the crowd gasped.

He thought, *I must look as fashionable as I've ever looked!*

But before he could address the crowd, a child shouted out, "He doesn't have anything on!"

Symptom #1: Dependability on Government Plans

In the last chapter, we mentioned America's Retirement Income Crisis and its symptoms. In this chapter, we're going to discuss Symptom #1: Dependability on Government Plans.

Even though he couldn't see them, the Emperor was led to believe the clothing he purchased (and was wearing) was real.

We have been led to believe that modern retirement planning has adequately replaced traditional retirement planning, but like those clothes the Emperor "wore", these government plans aren't always what they seem.

But before we get into that, let's compare the way America used to retire, to the way America has been retiring since the 1980s.

Picture a three-legged stool.

If traditional retirement income resembles a three-legged stool, one leg represents your pension, one represents social security, and the third is your non-market based personal savings.

Today, those legs are slightly different. Social security remains, but 'pensions' have been replaced with '401(k)s', and 'personal savings' is now a blend of cash and 'diversified' brokerage accounts.

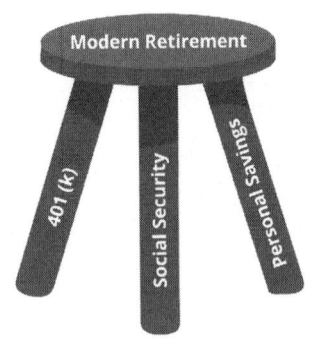

[Illustration: Modern Retirement stool with legs labeled "401(k)", "Social Security", and "Personal Savings"]

But the problem with this picture is that even though the stools look basically the same, they're dramatically different.

On the Traditional Retirement Stool, from nuts to bolts, the pension leg is managed by your employer. All you do is decide how much to contribute each paycheck.

The Modern Retirement Stool is different. The 401(k) leg is managed primarily by you. Your employer manages the contribution you chose and the relationship with the account vendor, but you decide how the money is invested. When you sign up for a 401(k), you have to decide which stocks, bonds, and/or mutual funds to invest in.

Does your 401(k)plan come with a training video on how to do that?

Of course not.

The modern stool may seem like it's replaced the traditional version, but it really hasn't.

This is a very powerful concept that I'll explain further in a moment, but first, I want to talk about the history of the pension, and America's transition to the 401(k).

> ## A Brief History of the Pension
>
> From before the turn of the 19th century until the 1980s, pensions were the standard retirement tool used by most American corporations.
>
> Called a **defined benefit plan**, they were fully managed by the employer and promised guaranteed income for life.
>
> They were meant to incentivize employees to stay loyal, and they worked. Back then, people stayed loyal to companies for decades. How many people do you know who worked for the same company for more than 30 years?
>
> But people started living longer (more on that later) and pensions began to get more and more expensive. It wasn't long before corporations started looking for more affordable alternatives.

Do You Have a 401(k)?

That affordable solution was the 401(k).

Do you have a 401(k)?

Your Government Plan Isn't What It Seems

If you don't, you probably know somebody who does, right?

Almost everywhere you go, on your first day of work, the HR representative passes you some paperwork, gives you a spiel about how important it is to save for retirement, and tells you the company will match what you contribute, up to a certain percentage.

That sounds like a pretty great deal, right?

So, you sign on the line, decide how much you want taken out of each paycheck, and never think about it again, right?

What if I told you the 401(k) was never meant to serve as a primary retirement income tool? I'll tell you more about that a little later. First, it's important to understand exactly where the 401(k) came from.

The United States Revenue Act of 1978

In 1978, congress passed the United States Revenue Act and added section 401(k) to the Internal Revenue Code. The provision allowed employees to put aside pre-tax dollars for retirement[15].

In 1980 a consultant petitioned the IRS to alter section 401(k) of the code to include low-income employees.

They agreed, and he wrote a **defined contribution plan** based on the new 401(k) legislature.

Big companies offered them first, but it wasn't long before smaller companies (and companies who had never offered retirement plans before) started offering them as well.

Take a look at this chart.

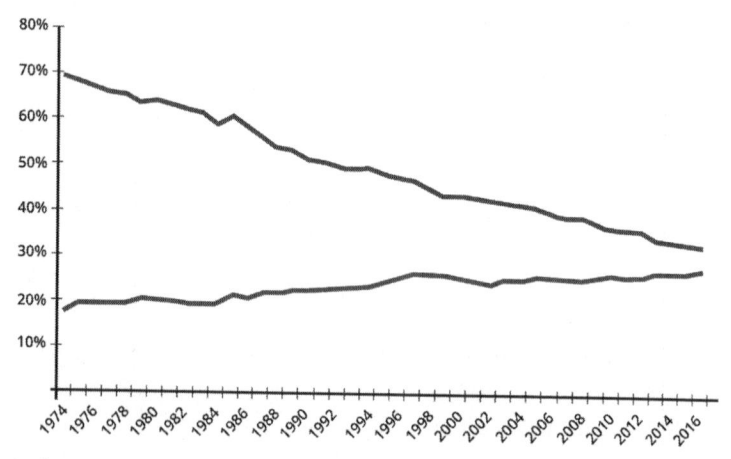

Top: Defined Benefit Plan (pension) vs Bottom: Defined Contribution Plan (401(k))

In 1979, just under 70% of private sector working Americans relied on a defined benefit plan to retire, compared to only about 13% today.

The 401(k) has no doubt replaced the pension...but is that a good thing?

The founders of the 401(k) don't think so. Ted Benna, the consultant who petitioned the IRS, now says the 401(k) will fail many Americans in retirement[16].

The Shift to the 401(k)

In the 1980s, America began shifting away from pensions and toward 401(k)s.

For employers, the benefits were obvious. They were much more affordable than pensions and saved big corporations millions (if not *billions*). And it allowed smaller companies to be competitive. By offering defined contribution plans, they were able to compete with the plans offered by large companies. The talent scouts playing field had been leveled.

But the benefits for employees are much harder to see. For one, they are riskier. Defined *benefit* plans provided guaranteed income for life, defined *contribution* plans are tied to the stock market, and are subject to losses[17].

Many Americans don't know or understand that.

Who Can Say No to Free Money?

The 401(k) was never originally designed to replace the pension; It was only meant to supplement it.

Pensions were getting more and more expensive, and the 401(k) was originally added to the Internal Revenue Code for high-earning employees as a way to set extra, tax-deferred cash.

When the IRS agreed to Benna's petition, everything changed. The 401(k) caught on like wildfire because not only could employees put aside pre-tax money (and possibly lower their tax bracket), many companies offered a match, agreeing to pay up to a certain percentage into the employee's account.

They were offering "free money"...and, who can say no to free money?

The IRS recognized their mistake and in the late 1980s, tried to invalidate 401(k) plans, twice. They were concerned that the tax income the government received would drop too much if too many people converted to 401(k) retirement plans too quickly.

But their attempts were unsuccessful, and the 401(k) took over.

Like we talked about earlier in this chapter, just about everyone today has a 401(k). Unfortunately, it isn't an adequate substitute for the pension. It may *look* like it is, but remember, things aren't always as they seem.

In my opinion, the modern retirement stool should look more like this:

[Stool diagram: "True Modern Retirement" supported by three legs labeled "401(k)", "Social Security", and "Personal Savings"]

Social Security Isn't the Same

The constant leg on both stools is social security...or is it?

Social security isn't what it used to be, and it isn't going to be anything like it is now. Like the 401(k), you might even say social security isn't what it seems...

What is social security?

> Social security is a retirement system run by the Social Security System, a federal organization. It was initiated by President Franklin D. Roosevelt in 1935 to help Americans recover from the devastating effects of the Great Depression, when millions of people lost their jobs and many elderly people were left without a source of income.

Originally, social security benefits were only granted to retirees and some unemployed people and were meant to provide temporary relief.

It was also designed to cover a very small population of people. In 1945, 42 people contributed to the program for every 1 person in need.

Today, social security is much different. It covers a much larger percentage of the population. In 2013, there were only 2.9 people working for every single person collecting social security[18].

Worker-to-Beneficiary Ratio, Selected Years 1960–2060

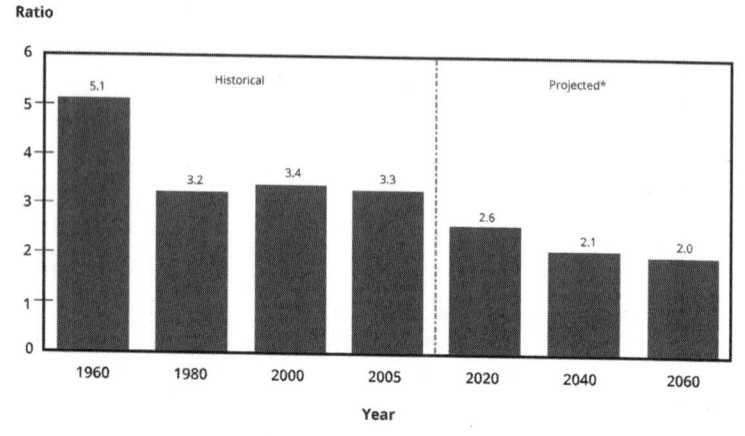

Year	Ratio
1960	5.1
1980	3.2
2000	3.4
2005	3.3
2020	2.6
2040	2.1
2060	2.0

(1960–2005: Historical; 2020–2060: Projected*)

SOURCE: Board of Trustees (2006, Table IV.B2), projected using the intermediate assumptions in the 2006 annual report of the Board of Trustees of the Federal Old-Age and Survivors Insurance and Disability Insurance Trust Funds.

How and *when* did it change?

An Aging Population

The answer isn't simple.

When social security was introduced in 1935, the life expectancy was 60 years old for males and 64 for females. The benefit age was set at 66, which assumed that most people would be dead by the time they qualified for social security.

Compare that to life expectancy today, where males are expected to reach 77 and females, 81[19].

Because we're living longer, social security is getting more expensive to maintain, per person.

And the future of social security doesn't look much better. If anything, it looks worse.

Birth rates in the U.S. have been declining since the 1970s, meaning the population overall is aging.

Birth rates, Selected Years 1946–2030

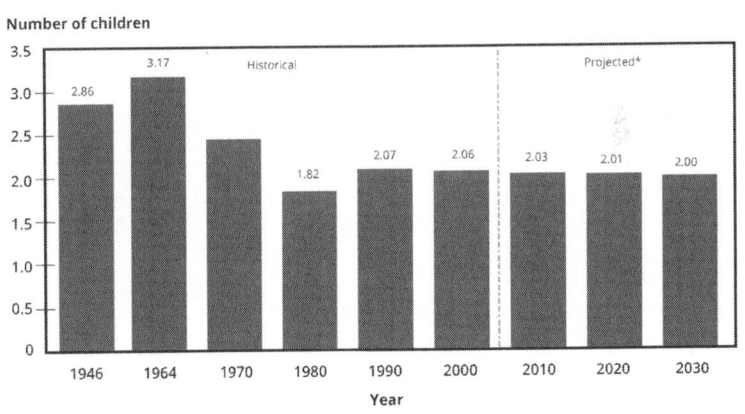

Number of children

Year	Number of children
1946	2.86
1964	3.17
1970	(Historical)
1980	1.82
1990	2.07
2000	2.06
2010	2.03
2020	2.01
2030	2.00

SOURCE: Board of Trustees (2006, Table V.A1), projected using the intermediate assumptions in the 2006 annual report of the Board of Trustees of the Federal Old-Age and Survivors Insurance and Disability Insurance Trust Funds.

Only 12% of the population is 65 and older today, but by 2080, it is projected to be 23%.

Low birth rates are also causing the working-age population to shrink from 60% today to a projected 54% in 2080[20].

An aging America means fewer workers to support a growing, retired population.

Take a look at the chart below. It depicts America's population in the thousands separated first by decade, then by age.

As you can see, the percentage of the older population (age 65+) increases with every decade. The population is getting older, meaning the working population is decreasing. It's undeniable.

U.S. Population By Age, Selected Years 1950-2080

Year	Population (thousands)	Percentage 65 or older			
	All ages	Under 20	20-64	65 or older	
Historical					
1950	160,118	54,466	92,841	12,811	8
1970	214,765	80,684	113,158	20,923	10
1990	260,458	75,060	153,368	32,029	12
2005	302,323	83,963	181,457	36,902	12
Projected					
2020	339,269	87,547	198,213	53,510	16
2040	376,856	92,268	207,416	77,172	20
2060	402,079	96,760	218,777	86,543	22
2080	428,214	101,159	230,137	96,918	23

SOURCE: Board of Trustees (2006, Table V.A2) and authors' calculations. NOTE: For the purpose of this table, the U.S. population is the Social Security area population, comprising residents of the 50 states and the District of Columbia (adjusted for net census undercount)' civilian residents of Puerto Rico, the Virgin Islands, Guam, American Samoa, and the Northern Mariana Islands; federal civilian employees and persons in the armed forces abroad and their dependents; crew members of merchant vessels; and all other U.S. citizens abroad, projected using the intermediate assumptions in the 2006 annual report of the Board of Trustees of the Federal Old-Age and Survivors Insurance and Disability Insurance Trust Funds.

Strategies Designed to Protect Your Retirement

When it comes to your retirement, like the *Emperor's New Clothes*, things most certainly aren't as they seem.

An aging population means the social security benefit fund is shrinking...rapidly.

Starting in 2035, the Social Security Administration website states that the government will only be able to pay 75% of social security benefits.

> *"Currently, the Social Security Board of Trustees projects program cost to rise by 2035 so that taxes will be enough to pay for only 75 percent of scheduled benefits.*[21]*"*

Unless major changes are made before 2037, the government is scheduled to reduce social security payments by 24%. In 17 short years, the $1,368/month you receive in social security benefits is scheduled to drop to $1026.

Can you live off that?

Thinking back to that three-legged stool, do you still think the social security legs should be the same? Shouldn't the Modern Retirement Stool look more like this?

True Modern Retirement
(Social Security & 401 (K))

[Diagram of a three-legged stool labeled "True Modern Retirement" with legs labeled "401 (k)", "Social Security", and "Personal Savings Brokerage Account"]

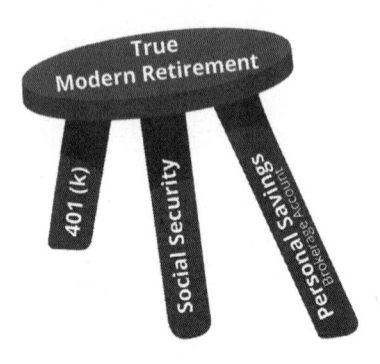

That's pretty lopsided, right?

You have been led to believe that the way we retire today is as secure as the way we retired yesterday, but I have shown you quite the opposite.

The 401(k) was never intended to replace the pension, yet that is what it has done. Once, America relied on defined benefit plans with guaranteed income for life. Today, we rely on defined contribution plans tied to market volatility and subject to loss. When the market crashed in 2008, some people lost as much as 40% of their retirement savings.

I've also shown you that social security isn't what it seems. You won't be able to rely on it to support your retirement income, because the nation is aging too quickly. The fund is depleting rapidly and who knows if our government can do anything to bring it back.

But if you're relying on that Modern Retirement Stool, the stool supported primarily by government dependent plans, I'm here to tell you there's hope. Like I mentioned earlier in this chapter, there are tools and strategies out there designed to protect your retirement and make your retirement stool sturdier (plus possibly give you income for life).

I'm sure some of you think the solution is your brokerage account…

But remember Retirement Income Crisis Symptom #2? Market losses and opportunity costs.

In the next chapter, I'm going to tell you how much money you're really losing in the market.

It's probably a lot more than you think.

Chapter Four:

How Much Does Market Loss Really Cost?

Black Monday was a big day in America's financial history. It marked the beginning of the Great Depression.

Let me back up a few days to October 24 and 25, 1929, otherwise known as **Black Thursday** and **Black Friday.** Over these two days, 13 million shares were traded. People were panicked, and the market began to fall.

On October 29, 1929, Black Monday, banks around the country shut down. These financial institutions had borrowed stock (and accepted stock) for margin trading[22]. Dips in the market directly affected their cash flow.

The general public knew this, so when the market started to crash on October 24th, 1929, people ran to the banks to withdraw their money. They were afraid the bank would shut down and they would lose their money forever.

The banks simply didn't have the money, so they shut down[23]. On the worst day, the Dow Jones dropped 13%. The Great Depression had officially begun.

It also marked the beginning of a massive **bear market** (a market with falling prices). The S&P 500 fell 86% in 34 months and didn't get back to its previous peak until 1954[24].

It took *22 years* for the market to come back to where it was before the bear market, before the stock prices began to fall. That's a really long time.

A crash like that (with a recovery period of 22 years) probably isn't going to happen in our lifetime, but anytime the market loses value, it takes time to recover.

Since World War II, there have been 11 bear markets.

Bear Market	Duration (Months)	% Decline	Years Needed to Breakeven
Sept. '29-June'32	33	86.7	25.2
July'33-Mar'35	20	33.9	2.3
Mar'37-Mar'38	12	54.5	8.8
Nov'38-Apr'42	41	45.8	6.4
May'46-Mar'48	22	28.1	4.1
Aug'56-Oct'57	14	21.6	2.1
Dec'61-June'62	6	28	1.8
Feb'66-Oct'66	8	22.2	1.4
Nov'68-May'70	18	36.1	3.3
Jan'73-Oct'74	21	24.2	7.6
Nov'80-Aug'82	21	27.1	2.1
Aug'87-Dec'87	4	33.5	1.9
July'90-Oct'90	3	19.9	0.6
Mar'00-Mar'03	35	49.2	4.7

Image courtesy of www.mooncap.com

In 1973, when the Dow fell 45%, losses were not recovered until 1982. That's *96 months*, the longest recovery period in history. The shortest on record happened in 1980; it only took three months to recover. The average recovery period is about 15 months, which is still a long time[25].

Can you afford to take a break from saving for retirement for 15 months?

Symptom #2: Market Loss and Opportunity Costs

Market loss and **opportunity costs** is the second symptom of America's Retirement Income Crisis. Many of the people I talk to don't understand either of those terms.

Let's start with market loss. Most investors assume that it takes the same percentage gain to make up for a loss. For example, if you lose 50%, it takes a 50% gain to win it all back.

But that's wrong. In fact, it takes a *bigger* gain to make up for that loss.

For example, if you have $100 invested and you lose 50%, you now have $50, right?

But if you gain 50% on that $50, you only earn $25.

Are you whole?

No. You're only up to $75, meaning you're still $25 short.

If you lose 50% in the market, you need a 100% gain to earn it all back.

Anytime you lose money in the market, you need a *higher* return to break even. That's why it takes so long for the market to recover from a major crash.

Take a look at this chart to see what I mean.

The Amount that Must be Re-Earned to Fully Recover from a Stock Market Loss

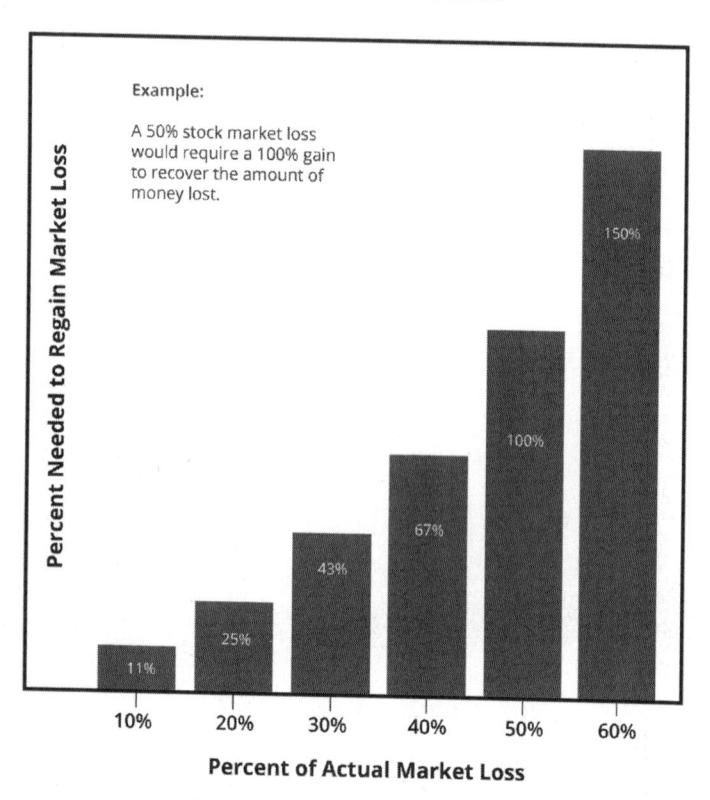

Example:

A 50% stock market loss would require a 100% gain to recover the amount of money lost.

Percent of Actual Market Loss	Percent Needed to Regain Market Loss
10%	11%
20%	25%
30%	43%
40%	67%
50%	100%
60%	150%

Image courtesy of www.marketwatch.com.

When you lose 50%, you need a 100% gain to break even. That's very difficult and almost impossible to do, which means getting your account back to even is going to take a very long time.

Let me give you an example. The 2000s may very well go into the history books as "The Lost Decade of Investing."

Have you heard of the "**Dot Com Bubble**"?

On March 27, 2000, the U.S. entered a bear market it took 31 months to recover from. The S&P 500 lost 49% of its value during that time.

Most of us are familiar with the stock market crash of 2007. The market had barely recovered from the Dot Com Bubble when it was hit again. This time the market dropped even more (a staggering 59%) before recovering 17 months later in 2009[26].

The Lost Decade, S&P 500 2000-2009

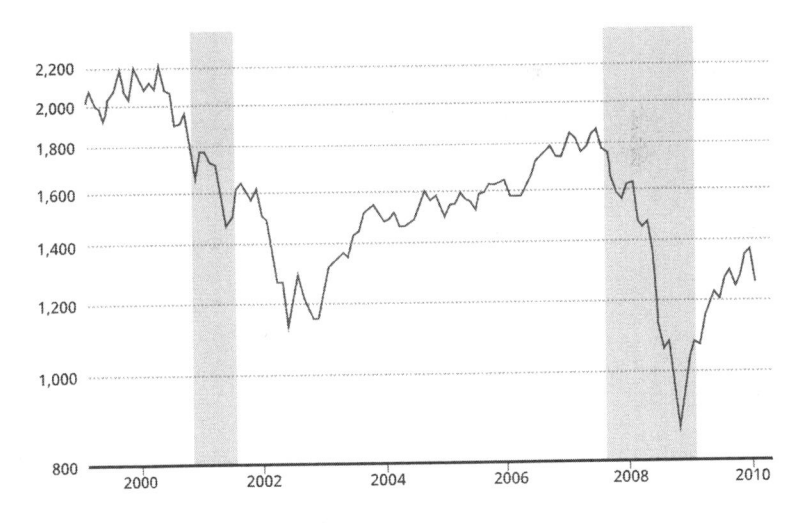

If you had invested $1 in the S&P 500 in 2000, you would have had $0.90 in 2009. After nearly a decade, you would have *lost* money.

The Road to Recovery

Recovering from market losses takes a lot longer than most people expect.

Is it possible to recover in a year?

Well, that really depends on how much you lose.

From 1970-2009, the single biggest S&P 500 return was 37.58% in 1995. According to Craig Israelsen's research below that return would have made up for 10% or 20% in losses the year before, but if the market took more than a 35% hit then recovering in a year would have been impossible.

Portfolio Loss	Gain Needed to Restore Loss	Percentage chance of recovery from loss within...					
		1 Year	2 Year	3 Year	4 Year	5 Year	10 Year
-10.0%	-11.1%	25.5%	74.4%	81.6%	78.4%	77.8%	93.5%
-20.0%	-25.0%	25.0%	48.7%	68.4%	67.6%	72.2%	93.5%
-35.0%	-54.0%	0.0%	17.9%	34.2%	56.8%	61.1%	93.5%
-50.0%	-100.0%	0.0%	0.0%	7.9%	13.5%	36.1%	80.6%
-65.0%	-186.0%	0.0%	0.0%	0.0%	2.7%	5.6%	61.3%

SOURCE: "The Match of Gains and Losses," Craig L. Israelsen, Ph. D., Woodbury School of Business, Utah Valley University, 2010.

Even if the market only takes a 10% hit, when we factor in historical data, there is only a 25.5% chance of recovering the following year.

Smaller losses can be resolved relatively quickly. There is a 25% chance of recovering from a 20% loss in one year, and a 93% chance of recovering within 10 years.

But let's dig a little deeper.

Looking at the table above, the S&P 500 index only has a 17.8% chance of gaining 54% over a two-year period to recover from a 35% loss. The probability increases to 34.2% in three years, 57% in four, and 61% in five. That means there is a 39% chance it will take more than five years to recover from a 35% loss.

More serious losses require even longer recovery time frames, if recovery is even possible. For example, if the S&P 500 drops 50% (like it did in 2008) there is a 0% chance of recovery within the first two years and only a 36% chance of recovery within a five-year period.

The True Cost of Market Losses

Market losses can be very costly. Getting your account back to where it was before the loss requires *additional* contributions. You can never recover your lost money; you can only replenish those losses with new money.

And if your money is lost, you can't earn interest on it.

We call those losses **opportunity costs**. When you lose a dollar, you don't just lose that dollar, you lose the potential interest that dollar would have earned if it had been invested.

Warren Buffett famously says:

> "Rule #1: Never lose money.
> Rule #2: Never forget Rule #1." [27]

He was referring to opportunity costs!

Let me give you some real-life examples:

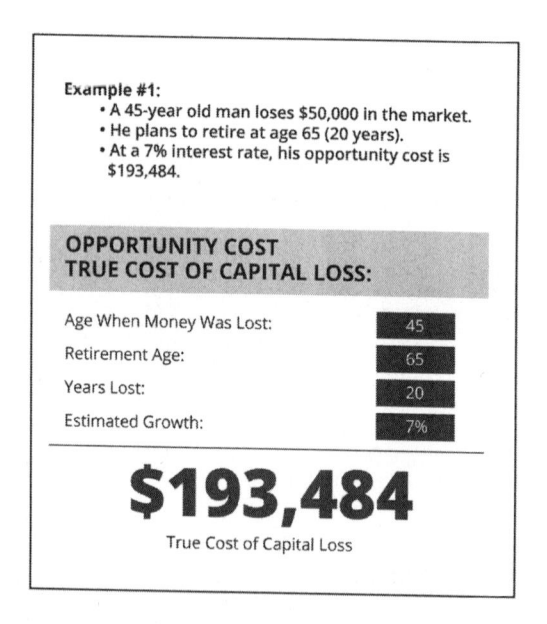

Example #1:
- A 45-year old man loses $50,000 in the market.
- He plans to retire at age 65 (20 years).
- At a 7% interest rate, his opportunity cost is $193,484.

OPPORTUNITY COST
TRUE COST OF CAPITAL LOSS:

Age When Money Was Lost:	45
Retirement Age:	65
Years Lost:	20
Estimated Growth:	7%

$193,484
True Cost of Capital Loss

Losing $50,000 in the market today, really means losing almost $200,000 20 years from now.

Let's take this a step further.

How Much Does Market Loss Really Cost?

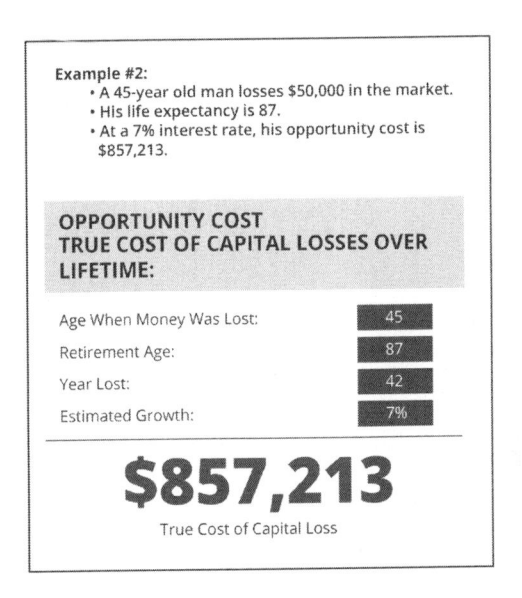

Example #2:
- A 45-year old man losses $50,000 in the market.
- His life expectancy is 87.
- At a 7% interest rate, his opportunity cost is $857,213.

OPPORTUNITY COST
TRUE COST OF CAPITAL LOSSES OVER LIFETIME:

Age When Money Was Lost:	45
Retirement Age:	87
Year Lost:	42
Estimated Growth:	7%

$857,213
True Cost of Capital Loss

If he didn't lose that money and he put it somewhere safe, where he could get 7% a year over his lifetime, assuming he lives up to age 87 then that $50,000 would grow to $857,000.

That's his lifetime loss. Not the original $50,000.

And that's only an initial loss of $50,000.

How much have you lost in the market?

A Misleading Average Return?

When I talk to people about investment options, I typically hear the following questions:

"What kind of return can you get me?"

"What was the average rate of return last year?"

"What is the average return for the last five years? How about the last ten?"

But the **average rate of return (ROR)** can be very misleading and doesn't mean anything if your principal isn't protected.

Here's a quick example for you:

Year	Market	Starting balance	Ending balance
1	100%	10,000	20,000
2	-50%	20,000	10,000
3	100%	10,000	20,000
4	-50%	20,000	10,000

The *average ROR* for this specific account is 25%.

If the average person saw that, he or she will think that there will be an extra 25% in the account...but in reality, there won't be any extra money.

This goes back to the fact that it takes a higher return to break even. That's why the average ROR can be misleading. In the example, our average ROR was 25% but because we had significant losses, we didn't have any extra money in our account.

Average Return vs. Average Compounding Return

There is also a difference between an **average** return and an **average compounding return.**

The chart below lists the annual S&P 500 return percentage over the last 20 years. To find the **average return** over the past 20 years, we simply add up all the percentages and divide by 20. That formula tells us the S&P 500 indexed had an average return of 7.47% from 1999 to 2018.

That's pretty good, right?

S&P Average Indexed Return, 1999-2018

Year	Return
2018	1.83%
2017	21.83%
2016	11.96%
2015	1.38%
2014	13.69%
2013	32.39%
2012	16.00%
2011	2.11%
2010	15.06%
2009	26.46%
2008	-37.00%
2007	5.49%
2006	15.79%
2005	4.91%
2004	10.88%
2003	28.68%
2002	-22.10%
2001	11.89%
2000	-9.10%
1999	21.04%
AVERAGE	7.47%

The problem is that the average return isn't revealing the **compound average return**, or the *real* rate of return.

To factor that rate, we compare the value of the S&P 500 in 1999 to the value of the S&P 20 years later.

Take a look at the chart below.

Annual Compounded Return

Inputs		
Present Value:	$	1229
Future Value:	$	2634
Years:		20

Results	
Compound Annual Growth Rat	3.89%

The average compounding return, from 1999 to 2018, is just under 4%.

That's very different than the 7.47%

Investor Psychology

Dalbar Inc. has studied investor behavior for decades. Their most recent report shows that over the past 30 years, the S&P 500 has done around 10%, but the average investor only saw 2-3% gains[28].

Any guesses as to why?

How Much Does Market Loss Really Cost?

Because no one has a crystal ball, no one can predict the future, and no one can outguess the casino.

If we keep our money in the market during a downturn, we might earn that 10% gain, but we don't because we're human! We get worried when we see our money disappearing!

When we see our money disappearing month after month, we pull it out of the market to stop the bleeding. It's hard to blame anyone for doing that because it's basic self-preservation.

Unfortunately, most people sell too late (like I mentioned, none of us have a crystal ball and none of us can see the future) and then when the market rebounds, most of us are sitting on the sidelines, missing out on the big returns that typically follow a massive correction.

So, after watching the market perform in the double digits for a few years and experiencing the pain of 0% interest rates in our bank accounts, we put our money back in the market.

But now there's a new problem. The market is high, meaning we're at the top when the roller coaster starts to go back down. We buy high when we see the market is performing well and we sell low when we see our money disappearing.

This is why Dalbar shows the S&P 500 earned an average of 10% over the past 30-years, but the average guy only earned 2-3%.

A little later in this book, I will share with you a few strategies that will allow you to protect a portion of your money from those crashes. While everyone else is struggling to catch up and get back to even, you'll be ahead of the game. You'll be able to capture your gains and continue to grow your money.

Investor Psychology Cycle

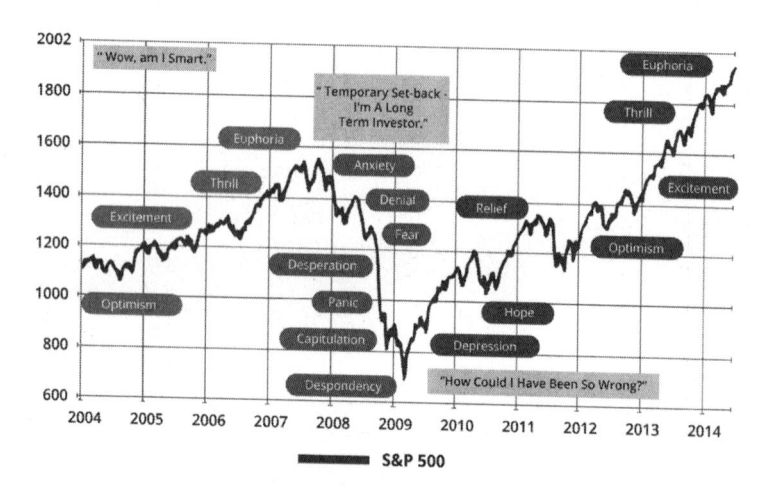

The Sequence of Returns Risk

We've talked about opportunity costs and how the average rate of return can be misleading, but if you're nearing or already in retirement, the **sequence of returns risk** is something that may permanently devastate your retirement savings.

No one can predict the market. We all know that.

It's one thing to fund your 401(k), experience a huge crash, and watch your account recover and continue to grow for the next 10 to 20 years.

But what happens when you retire and all of the sudden, BOOM, the market crashes and you lose 30%?

We talked about market recovery times. We also talked about how true recovery requires additional funds and that once dollars are lost, they're gone forever.

Retirees typically don't have the time to wait for the market to recover. It's also unlikely that they'll have access to additional cash.

And because retirees are withdrawing money from their market accounts to live on, their money is going to run out that much faster.

Take a look at the following example.

The Retirement Epidemic

Year	PORTFOLIO A Return	PORTFOLIO A Balance	PORTFOLIO B Return	PORTFOLIO B Balance
0		$100,000		$100,000
1	-15%	$80,750	22%	$115,900
2	-4%	$72,720	8%	$119,772
3	-10%	$60,948	30%	$149,204
4	8%	$60,424	7%	$154,298
5	12%	$62,075	18%	$176,171
6	10%	$62,782	9%	$186,577
7	-7%	$53,737	28%	$232,418
8	4%	$50,687	14%	$259,257
9	-12%	$40,204	-9%	$231,374
10	13%	$39,781	16%	$262,594
11	7%	$37,216	-6%	$242,138
12	-10%	$28,994	17%	$277,452
13	19%	$28,553	19%	$324,217
14	17%	$27,557	-10%	$287,296
15	-6%	$21,204	7%	$302,056
16	16%	$18,796	13%	$335,674
17	-9%	$12,555	-12%	$290,993
18	14%	$8,612	4%	$297,433
19	28%	$4,624	-7%	$271,962
20	9%	$0	10%	$293,658
21	18%	$0	12%	$323,297
22	7%	$0	8%	$343,761
23	30%	$0	-10%	$304,885
24	8%	$0	-4%	$287,890
25	22%	$0	-15%	$240,456

Arithmetic Mean	6.80%		6.80%
Standard Deviation	12.80%		12.80%
Compund Growth Rate	6.00%		6.00%

Both portfolios start out with $100,000 and withdraw $5,000 each year. In years 1-3, Portfolio A sees losses and Portfolio B sees gains.

Twenty years into retirement, Portfolio A runs out of money, but after 25-years, Portfolio B is left with approximately $240,000.

That's a massive, unpredictable difference.

The timing of the market is very important. It could mean the difference between running out of money or living the high life in retirement. That's why it's important to put your money into something that is conservative and always protected. Something predictable and something you can count on.

Americans already aren't saving enough for retirement. A market crash could devastate what little savings they *do* have.

Can you afford to take that risk?

Next, we're going to talk about the third symptom (and America's biggest retirement risk), future taxes.

Chapter Five:

Is This Your Biggest Retirement Risk?

I want to open this chapter by telling you about one of my clients, Jim.

Jim is a retired marine who lost a large chunk of his retirement savings in 2008 while serving overseas.

When he came to see me, he had earned it all back, but was anxious about losing it again. It was all sitting in a qualified, government plan that was not only tied to the market but was also subjected to taxes.

"I'm afraid of market volatility, but I'm also afraid of taxes. All of my retirement savings is tied up in tax-deferred accounts. If the tax rate is higher when it's time to take my money out of the account, I'm afraid I'm going to lose a significant portion of my savings, and then I won't be able to work! Is there anything I can do?"

Jim stared at me from across my desk, his eyes wrinkled with worry.

This man had worked hard his entire life and served our country proudly. But, he couldn't retire with peace of mind because a large amount of his wealth was taxable.

Jim wanted a more conservative, tax-advantaged option.

Fortunately, I was able to help him. We moved a portion of his money into an account that would allow it to grow tax-deferred and withdraw the money on tax-free basis.

Helping Jim felt really good. He served our country. He deserves a worry-free retirement like any hard-working American.

Symptom #3: Future Taxes

I think I've made it pretty clear just how dangerous the market can be to your retirement savings.

I've also made it clear that your qualified, government plan is tied to the market.

But did you know that your 401(k), 403(b), and/or IRA is tied to the government, too?

"Many people are nervous about retirement. People need to realize that a safe and secure retirement means having your own plan, one that does not rely on the government." - Ed Slott, CPA

What does Ed Slott, a well-known Certified Public Accountant (CPA) and financial advisor, mean by that?

We already know that he believes taxes are the single biggest retirement risk because they're unknown.

I believe he's right. That's why I've listed **future taxes** as Retirement Income Crisis Symptom #3.

The Seed and the Harvest

The solution to this problem is **tax diversification,** but before we get into that, we need to understand the difference between *pre-tax* (a.k.a. *tax deferred*) and *after-tax.*

I like to use a farming analogy to help people understand the difference.

Would you rather pay tax on the seed or the harvest?

Let me explain.

One day, a farmer went to town to buy seeds. He walked into the nursery and saw that the seeds were on sale! Today only, he could get the seeds tax-deferred. He could avoid paying taxes now and save that money.

At first, the farmer was overjoyed. He started picking out his seed packs, thinking about all the money he would save in taxes!

But then he stopped. There was some fine print on the sale sign. It read:

> *Instead of paying taxes on the seed today, you will pay taxes on your future harvest. By purchasing the seeds tax-deferred, you agree to these terms.*

The farmer scratched his head. That didn't seem right. The seeds in his hand were only worth about $20. The harvest was potentially worth a whole lot more! Sure, there was the *possibility* that the harvest would yield nothing, but that was a risk he was willing to take.

He paid full price for the seeds and walked out of the nursery.

If you were a farmer would you rather pay taxes on the seed, knowing exactly how much taxes you have to pay? Or would you rather gamble and wait until the end of the harvest season to find out how much you'll owe?

I think most of us would rather pay tax on the seed. It's a much smaller amount!

Yet, we don't use the same logic when it comes to retirement planning.

Most of us rely on 401(k)s and IRAs, qualified, *pre-tax* government plans, to retire.

Sound familiar?

The contributions into a 401(k) are deposited *before* the government withholds any taxes. The money then grows tax-deferred, but all withdrawals are fully taxable at distribution.

When it comes to 401(k) plans, Americans are paying tax on the harvest, not the seed.

Would you rather pay taxes *before* you deposit it into a retirement account? Or would you rather pay taxes *later*, after your money has grown and compounded for decades?

Does Tax-Deferred Mean Tax-Free?

Most of us have (or have had), tax-deferred 401(k)s 403(b)s, and/or IRAs.

These plans are funded with *pre-tax* dollars.

But *pre-tax* doesn't mean *tax-free*.

Many people don't know the difference.

Do you?

I have found that most people forget the withdrawals from these accounts are taxed as ordinary income.

Pre-tax (or tax-deferred) means that both the assessment and payment of taxes is put off until a later date.

Tax-free means taxes are never paid.

Your 401(k), 403(b), and IRA aren't tax-free, they're tax-deferred. You have to pay taxes on the money in those accounts, eventually.

Are Tax-Deferrals a Good Thing?

Most people have been advised that tax-deferrals are a good thing.

Why?

The biggest sell is that tax-deferred contributions help lower your overall taxable income today.

And we all want to pay less in taxes, right?

Everything we do we are taxed. When we make money, the government takes some of it away, when we make a purchase, the government takes some of it away. Even when we die, the government taxes us!

> It makes sense that we want to avoid paying taxes. That might be why the standard advice is to maximize contributions to tax-deferred accounts.

For one, you save on taxes today by deferring the taxes on your 401(k) contributions. You can also possibly lower your annual tax bracket and see overall tax breaks.

What's not to love?

Conventional Wisdom

It sounds like a good deal, right? Our contributions are tax-deductible, and the investment earnings accumulate inside the plan without an immediate tax consequence.

Our overall income is also lowered, potentially dropping us into a lower tax bracket.

Tax savings all around!

Right?

At least, that's what conventional wisdom tells us.

This problem is compounded by the mistaken idea that a big retirement fund of tax-deferred income means you have created wealth.

Instead, you have created a tax liability over which you will have little if any control.

Wealth is not created within tax-deferred retirement accounts; It is created by investing after-tax dollars.

But, like we talked about in Chapter Three, the majority of Americans have been using these qualified, government accounts to plan for retirement since the 1980s.

If offered by our employer, first we contribute all long-term savings, such as retirement savings, to a 401(k), and if we're lucky our employer has a company match. Then we contribute any other available funds to a Roth IRA.

In general, this is good advice.

However, many investors <u>maximize their 401(k) above the employer match</u> for the sole purpose of reducing current taxable income (like we just mentioned).

Is This Your Biggest Retirement Risk?

Some of them also invest in a traditional IRA, instead of the Roth IRA, for the same reason (current tax savings).

These are both mistakes for a large portion of your money.

For one, your social security payments are directly tied to the income you earned during your working years. The less money you contribute, the less money you'll have down the road.

And maybe more importantly, all that money will have to be *taxed*. The more tax-deferred income you contribute to a qualified plan (of any kind), the more you will be taxed on in retirement.

Rather than pay tax on the seed, 91% of Americans follow conventional wisdom and pay taxes on the harvest.

And, it's understandable. Retirement seems so far away...and many need the extra money *now*.

But as we know, the day will come when taxes will be due on both the contributions and the investment earnings inside your qualified, government plan.

For some, it will likely come when you retire. For others, it will be when the government forces you to withdraw money from your plan.

> **Do you think you can keep your tax-deferred money inside your 401(k) or IRA forever?**
>
> When you reach 70.5, you <u>must</u> withdraw your money, regardless of market performance or the current tax rate. The law requires it.
>
> So, whether you like it or not, eventually you <u>will</u> have to pay taxes on the money in your 401(k), 403(b), and/or IRA.
>
> Remember, tax-deferred doesn't mean tax-free.

A Lower Tax Bracket?

Still think tax-deferrals are a good thing?

Many of you are still convinced they are because you assume you will be in a lower tax bracket when you retire.

But, will you?

A lot of the tax breaks you receive while working go away in retirement.

Your mortgage is a tax deduction, but typically, the house is paid off in retirement.

Right?

The lack of deductions really does add up and many retirees may wind up paying more taxes than they saved when they were working.

But regardless of tax deductions, if taxes go up, most Americans will end up paying more in taxes in retirement *anyway*. You might be in a lower tax bracket, but if taxes *double*, you're still going to pay more than you are today.

How Would You Feel if Taxes Doubled?

I believe taxes are going to go up.

Just how high?

According to David Walker, former U.S. Comptroller General, based on the current fiscal path, in order for our country to avoid bankruptcy, future taxes will have to *double*[29].

Double!

The Congressional Budget Office conducted their own study and are also predicting that taxes will double[30].

Can you imagine if federal, state, and local taxes double?

And what if it doesn't stop there?

We are taxed on everything. When we stay in a hotel, we're typically charged a room tax. When we buy groceries, or clothing, we pay sales tax.

What if those taxes start to double, too?

If they double, how long will it take?

The Congressional Budget Office predicts it might happen in as little as 10-15 years. If Social Security and Medicare go unchanged, they predict the lowest bracket will increase from 10% to 25%, the 25% bracket wise rise to 63%, and the highest bracket will climb from 39% to 88%.

	Today	10-15 Years in the Future
Tax Bracket 1	10%	25%
Tax Bracket 2	25%	63%
Tax Bracket 3	39%	88%

If you have to pay taxes in retirement, including on your retirement income, because we don't know the future of taxation, you could end up paying two to three times more in taxes in retirement than you would have in your working years.

Ed Slott, a CPA and one of the nation's leading tax experts, says, "taxes are your single biggest retirement risk"...

And he's right.

We don't know what the future tax rates will be, and that's a problem.

Will Taxes Be Lower or Higher?

If taxes go up, it is very likely that you might end up paying *more* in taxes when you retire.

Many of you reading this are shaking your heads because you're convinced that you will be paying less in taxes because you'll be in a lower tax bracket.

You might be right; I don't know your specific situation.

But even if you *are*, if your savings is tied to a qualified, government plan, you're still going to run into trouble when you need to withdraw your tax-deferred money.

Why?

Because most people agree taxes will likely be higher in the future.

Do you?

If you don't, have you considered our country's growing deficit?

> Currently, we are more than $21 *trillion* dollars in debt, a number that's growing rapidly.

To top it off, we have future social programs to pay for. The Peterson Foundation audited financial statements and calculated the federal government accumulated $56.4 *trillion* in "total liabilities and unfunded promises" for Medicare and Social Security.

The debt is growing so quickly, there is a website designed to track it: www.USDebtClock.org.

US Debt Clock.org

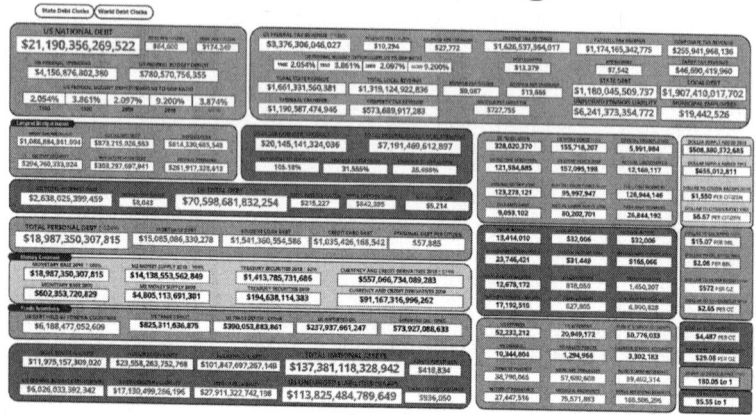

If you aren't alarmed by the state of our growing national deficit, spend a few minutes visiting this site and you very well might be.

This is a lot to take in...but the main number to focus on is that $21 trillion in debt. It's hard to imagine, right?

And there isn't a lot of green, is there?

Is it easier to picture $483,000 per American household?

We are beholden to this debt. Whether we like it or not, we share a very large share of the government's financial burden.

And just how likely do you think it is that we will ever be able to pay it back?

In order to fully analyze our country's debt, the national debt by year needs to be compared to the size of the economy. We can use GDP (gross domestic product) to measure the economy, giving us the GDP to debt ratio.

Take a look at the chart below, prepared by the Congressional Budget Office in 2014[31]. As you can see, in 1946 our GDP to debt ratio was the highest in history at 106%. In 2014, it was 76%, and in 2017, it reached 104%[32].

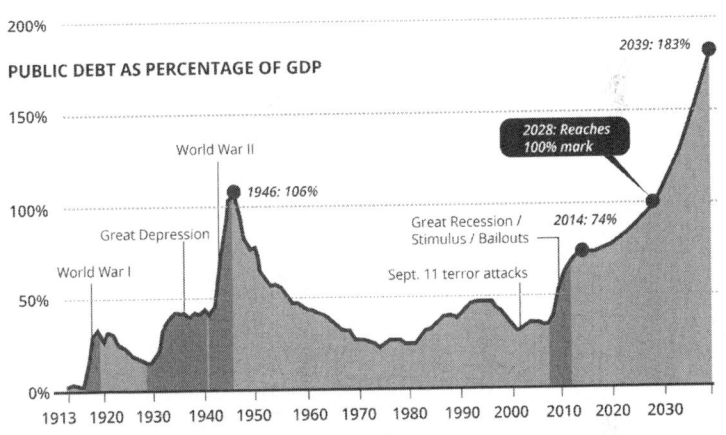

PUBLIC DEBT AS PERCENTAGE OF GDP

- World War I
- Great Depression
- World War II
- 1946: 106%
- Sept. 11 terror attacks
- Great Recession / Stimulus / Bailouts
- 2014: 74%
- 2028: Reaches 100% mark
- 2039: 183%

Publicly Held Debt Set to Skyrocket
Runaway spending on Medicare, Medicaid, and Social Security will drive federal debt to an unsustainable level over the next few decades. Total national debt comprises publicly held debt (the most relevant to credit markets) and debt that one part of the government owes to another, such as the Social Security Trust Fund.

Why are these numbers important? Let's find out.

The Government Controls the Tax Code

The government controls the tax code and can change it anytime.

Historically, we are in comparatively low tax rates; today, the top income tax is 35%.

If you go back to 1986, the top rate was 50%, and a decade before that, it was 70%. The highest tax bracket in our country's history was post-WWII, when the top rate was 94%. That also happens to be when the GDP to debt ratio was the highest in our nation's history.

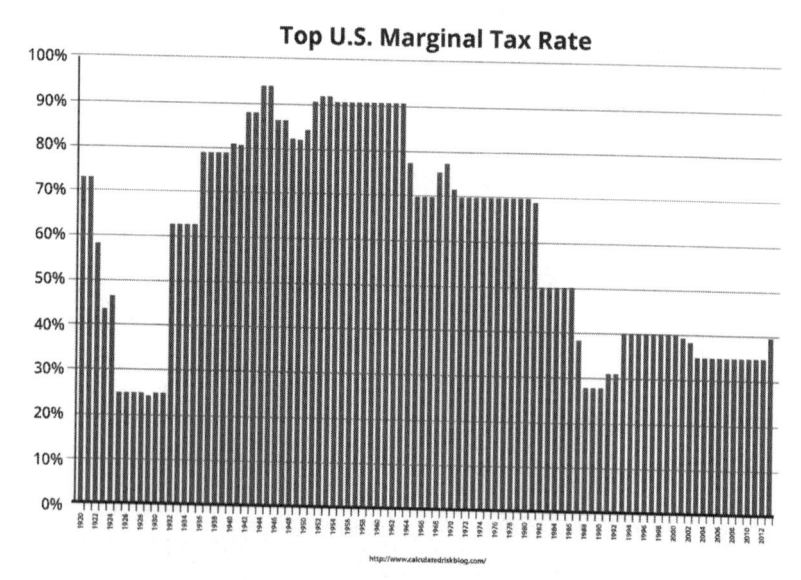

Top U.S. Marginal Tax Rate

https://www.calculatedriskblog.com/

Back to the current GDP to debt ratio. Like I mentioned in the previous section, just last year, it reached 104%. Do you think taxes will increase, too, just like they did in the mid-1940s?

I do.

No one knows what the future tax rates will be, but we do know that for the wealthiest, when the GDP to debt ratio was higher than 100%, it has been as high as 94%. We also know the government can change the tax code at any time.

The amount of tax you owe to the government is like the amount of debt you owe to the bank, and the interest rate is variable.

Do you really want your retirement income subjected to that kind of uncertainty?

Or, would you rather rely on a strategy that works independently of the government?

Is the Solution Tax Diversification?

Does your retirement plan include provisions to manage the impact of taxes?

If it doesn't, there's hope!

Like I mentioned earlier in the chapter, the solution is tax diversification.

What is tax diversification?

We hear a lot about the need for diversification when talking about our investments.

In the investment world, this most often refers to the idea that you shouldn't invest all of your money in one stock.

"You need to diversify. You need a blend of stocks, bonds, <u>and</u> mutual funds."

Most of us are very familiar with portfolio diversification when planning for retirement but have no idea how the concept applies to taxes.

Tax diversification means that every retirement savings portfolio should have accounts that have both *pre*-tax and *after*-tax money.

For example, if you have a qualified, government plan with pre-tax (tax-deferred) dollars attached, you should also have an account with after-tax dollars.

There are a few vehicles that allow you to pay tax now and are tax-free at distribution; The one you choose should be customized to your specific tax situation.

(I'll tell you the specifics later, but one tool I'm particularly fond of is tied to what many tax experts consider the "golden child of the tax code".)

No one knows exactly what his or her tax rate will be in retirement. It depends on so many things: income, family status, retirement benefits, and even government tax policy.

What can you do in the face of this uncertainty?

Tax diversification.

Inflation, interest rates are killing America's retirement plans, too. In the next chapter, I'm going to tell you how.

Chapter Six:
Inflation, Interest Rates, and Your Erroneous Nest Egg

The Big Mac Index

Have you heard of the Big Mac Index?

Created in 1986 by *The Economist* magazine, the Big Mac Index was originally intended to "demonstrate the purchasing power" between countries[33].

But in 2013, *Forbes* magazine used the index to demonstrate the rate of inflation and how it differs from rates being reported by the U.S. Government.

In 1996, the cost of a Big Mac was $2.36.

In 2013, the cost was $4.33.

That's an 83.5% increase!

But the U.S. Government isn't reporting that. According to the Consumer Price Index (CPI), the tool they use to measure inflation, the cost of a Big Mac in 2013 should only be $3.49.

They're a whole $0.84 off[34].

Does that have you worried?

Symptom #4: Inflation

Another key obstacle to your financial freedom is inflation, that's why it's symptom number four.

What is inflation?

In economics, inflation refers to "a persistent, substantial rise in the general level of prices related to an increase in the volume of money and resulting in the loss of value of currency"[35].

Basically, inflation devalues your money causing the cost of everything you buy, to go up.

If you save your money in low-interest bearing accounts, like a bank savings account, you're probably *losing* money.

Think about it.

Savings accounts have interest rates between 1-2%, but inflation is between at 3-4%.

And that's what the government is reporting. The Big Mac Index tells a different story.

With that in mind, it is absolutely essential that you get a reasonable rate of return on your money in order to outpace inflation.

The Rule of 72

Albert Einstein discovered the **Rule of 72** and considered it his greatest discovery. (Yes, even over E=MC2[36].)

The rule is used to determine how long it will take an investment to double; simply divide 72 by the interest rate.

For example, if you are receiving a 3% return on your investment, when you apply the rule, you can expect your investment to double in 24 years.

Many people use the rule regularly to see what the value of their money will be in the future...

$$\frac{72}{\text{Rate of Return}} = \text{Time for Investment to Double}$$

Interest Rate	Years to Double
1%	72
2%	36
3%	24
4%	18
5%	14
6%	12
7%	10.3
8%	9
9%	8
10%	7.2
11%	6.5
12%	6
13%	5.5
14%	5.1
15%	4.8

But what most don't know is that the rule can also be used to determine how inflation will impact future purchasing power[37].

$$\frac{72}{\text{Inflation}} = \text{Time it takes for the Value of money to be cut in half}$$

Interest Rate	Years to Be Cut in Half
1%	72
2%	36
3%	24
4%	18
5%	14
6%	12
7%	10.3
8%	9
9%	8
10%	7.2
11%	6.5
12%	6
13%	5.5
14%	5.1
15%	4.8

To put this in real terms, let's say the inflation rate being reported is 4% and you currently need $100,000 a year to support your lifestyle.

In 18 years, your $100,000 will be worth $50,000, your money will be worth *half* of what it is today.

Inflation is sneaky, and if you don't plan for it, can be absolutely devastating to your retirement.

Symptom #5: Interest Charges

In the last chapter, I mentioned that conventional wisdom tells us to contribute to our 401(k)s to save for retirement.

Conventional wisdom is also to blame for Symptom #5: Interest Charges.

Years ago, best-selling author R. Nelson Nash, did a study that on average determined most Americans pay 34.5% of their income on interest charges. (This includes interest on mortgages, student loans, credit cards, car loans, etc.[38]).

That's shocking, right?

Today, Americans are saddled with massive amounts of debt because conventional wisdom tells us to finance everything.

"Work hard and make monthly payments to banks and finance companies for the items you purchased on credit. Do this for the rest of your life."

So, we go out and purchase homes, boats, and cars on credit. We finance our children's education on credit. Some of us even finance our vacations.

Most Americans purchase something before they can afford to.

Interest Rate vs. Volume of Interest

I have found that most Americans don't understand interest rates. We purchase things we can't afford, and then don't understand how the financing works. We don't understand how much we'll actually owe.

That's because most of us don't know the difference between **interest rates** and the **volume of interest.**

Let's say the interest rate for a $25,000 car loan is 7% over five years or 60 months. The monthly payment is $495.

The interest rate is 7%, which makes you think you're going to pay 7% in interest, right?

Wrong. You'll actually end up paying closer to 19%.

How? By the time you pay off the loan (five years), the value of the car will have depreciated by $13,000. When combined with the interest you're paying on the loan, you'll see a total loss of $17,702.

After five years, the car you paid $29,702 for will be worth only $12,000.

Now, our interest rate may be listed at 7%, but after all costs are considered we're paying $4,702 in interest charges, which actually equates to a 18.8% interest rate!

Car Loan	$25,000
Terms	5 years or 60 months
Interest Rate	7%
Monthly Payment	$495
Re-pay Total	$29,702
Car Value after 5-Year Depreciation	$12,000
Interest Costs	$4,702
Depreciation Costs	$13,000
Total Loss	$17,702
Real Interest Rate Paid to Bank	18.8%

So, where did 18.8% come from?

If we add up all the interest paid over five years ($4,702) and divide that from $25,000 (the original loan amount), we get 18.8%.

That means that during the life of the loan, we end up paying almost 20% in interest. That's a fifth of the total value of the loan...and certainly not the 7% interest that we were told when we first financed the car.

Mortgages are even worse. At the end of a 30-year fixed mortgage, most people end up paying 100% of the principal in interest. And that's only if you've financed your house once. If you've taken out a second mortgage, you'll end up paying even more.

Think about all of that income being wasted on interest rates!

Is America's Debt Growing?

Most Americans don't understand how interest rates work...

And of course, our debt is growing.

It looks like a perfect storm is brewing...

We've already covered the government's massive debt ($20 trillion and counting), but Americans have a growing personal debt of our own.

In 2017, Americans' total credit card debt reached an estimated $905 billion, almost an 8% increase from 2016[39]. The average household carries a credit card balance of $15,654, resulting in hundreds of dollars of annual interest.

And when you add in mortgages, student loans, and other debt (including medical expenses, a growing trend), the average household owes $131,431[40]. If the average interest rate is 5% (which is a very low average), that means the average household pays $6,571.55 a year in interest.

That's a lot!

Debt Balances and Trends

Type of debt	Total owed by average U.S. household carrying this type of debt	Total debt owed by U.S. consumers
Credit cards	$15,654	$905 billion
Mortgages	$173,995	$8.74 trillion
Auto loans	$27,669	$1.21 trillion
Student loans	$46,597	$1.36 trillion
Any type of debt	$131,431	$12.96 trillion

SOURCE: Federal Reserve Bank of New York, Center for Microeconomic Data

Take a look at the charts below to view other debt balances and trends.

At A Glance: U.S. Household Debt Trends

Type of debt	Change from Q1 2017 to Q2 2017
Mortgage debt	+0.78%
Auto loan debt	+2%
Student loan dept	No change
Credit card debt	+2.6%
Total household debt	+0.9%

SOURCE: *Federal Reserve Bank of New York, Center for Microeconomic Data*

How Does a Bank Make Money?

How would you like to avoid paying interest on major purchases?

I'll tell you how in a minute, but before I do, I want to talk about banks.

If you look at the largest companies in the world, the majority of them are banks.

And there is a reason for that.

If you're on the right side of the equation, banking can be a very lucrative business. Unfortunately, most of us consumers always end up on the wrong side.

The World's Largest Public Companies

Rank	Company	Country	Sales	Profits	Assets	Market Values
1	ICBC	China	$134.8 B	$37.8 B	$2,813.5 B	$237.3 B
2	China Construction Bank	China	$113.4 B	$30.6 B	$2,241 B	$202 B
3	JPMorgan Chase	United States	$108.2 B	$21.3 B	$2,359.1 B	$194.4 B
4	General Electric	United States	$147.4 B	$13.6 B	$685.3 B	$243.7 B
5	Exxon Mobil	United States	$420.7 B	$44.9 B	$333.8 B	$400.4 B
6	HSBC Holdings	United Kingdom	$104.9 B	$14.3 B	$2,684.1 B	$201.3 B
7	Royal Dutch Shell	Netherlands	$467.2 B	$26.6. B	$360.3 B	$213.1 B
8	Agricultural Bank of China	China	$103 B	$23 B	$2,124.2 B	$150.8 B
9	Berkshire Hathaway	United States	$162.5 B	$14.8 B	$427.5 B	$252.8 B
9	PetroChina	China	$308.9 B	$18.3 B	$347.8 B	$261.2 B
11	Bank of China	China	$98.1 B	$22.1 B	$2,033.8 B	$131.7 B
12	Wells Fargo	United States	$91.2 B	$18.9 B	$1,423 B	$201.3 B
13	Chevron	United States	$222.6 B	$26.2 B	$233 B	$232.5 B
14	Volkswagen Group	Germany	$254 B	$28.6 B	$408.2 B	$94.4 B
15	Apple	United States	$164.7 B	$41.7 B	$196.1 B	$416.6 B

Do you know how banks make money?

When you deposit $100, the bank gives you 1% interest to hold that money. If you don't withdraw a penny, you'll have $101 at the end of the year, right?

But the bank has bigger plans for your $100. They will take it and loan it out to someone who needs a mortgage, student loan, car loan, etc., and charge 5% interest.

The bank just made 4% loaning out your money.

There are strategies you can leverage that allow you to become your own bank. Later on in this book, I will show you how you can avoid interest charges and borrow from yourself (while your money potentially grows and grows).

Symptom #6: Your Erroneous Nest Egg

The sixth and final symptom of America's Retirement Income Crisis is the erroneous nest egg.

Most people I talk to believe that growing their nest egg is the best way to plan for retirement…but there is a big difference between your nest egg and your cash flow.

For example, your nest egg isn't going to pay off your mortgage because no one takes a "net worth statement" on your balance sheet as legal tender.

We have to pay with physical money, meaning people in retirement need **cash flow**.

In order to maintain a good standard of living throughout retirement, we need to focus on cash flow. Every day, we spend real cash on gas, food, utilities, vacations, clothes, etc. That nest egg balance sheet won't help with any of that.

It's all about consistent, monthly cash flow, regardless of whether or not you're working.

Every month, I speak with hundreds of people, and it seems like everyone has number.

"I want my nest egg to have $1 million."

"I think $2 million sounds about right."

"A $3 million nest egg should cut it."

Let me show you what I mean.

John Doe has $1 million saved and plans to withdraw 4% each year in retirement.

(For the sake of this example, I'm keeping the withdrawal rate simple and following the **rule of 4%**, which states that you should be able to remove 4% from your nest egg every year without running out of income.)[41]

Four percent of a million dollars is $40,000, so that's what John withdraws from his nest egg.

But he has to pay taxes now. If he pays 30% in taxes, he's left with about $28,000, or $2,333 a month in retirement.

Nest Egg	$1,000,000
Annual Withdrawal Rate	4%
Annual Income Before Taxes	$40,000
Annual Income After Taxes (30%)	$28,000
Monthly Income After Taxes (30%)	$2,333

Inflation, Interest Rates, and Your Erroneous Nest Egg

A million-dollar nest egg will produce less than $2,500 a month in retirement.

Is that enough?

For most of us, less than $2,500 a month simply isn't. That's why we have to focus on cash flow. A nest egg is a good thing to have, but most Americans don't understand that after taxes, year after year, a million dollars really doesn't get you very much.

And what if market crashes like it did in 2008 and drops by 40%?

Now, John's million-dollar nest egg is only worth $600,000. A 4% withdrawal is now $24,000, and after taxes (at 30%) he will likely be left with about $17,000 a year, or $1,400 a month.

Nest Egg	$600,000
Annual Withdrawal Rate	4%
Annual Income Before Taxes	$24,000
Annual Income After Taxes (30%)	$16,800
Monthly Income After Taxes (30%)	$1,400

Do you still think your nest egg will provide you with enough cash flow in retirement?

The amount of money you have in your "nest egg" isn't as important as your monthly (and annual) cash flow.

What type of cash flow do you need? Well, that's completely up to your unique situation and the strategy that works best for you.

3 Types of Cash Flow

Instead of focusing on your nest egg, you should be focusing on cash flow.

There are three different types of cash flow:

#1) **Passive Cash Flow** is regular, consistent income that requires little to no effort to maintain.

#2) **Guaranteed Cash Flow** is money that you will receive for the rest of your life, no matter how long you live.

#3 **Tax-Free Cash Flow** is money that isn't subjected to taxes.

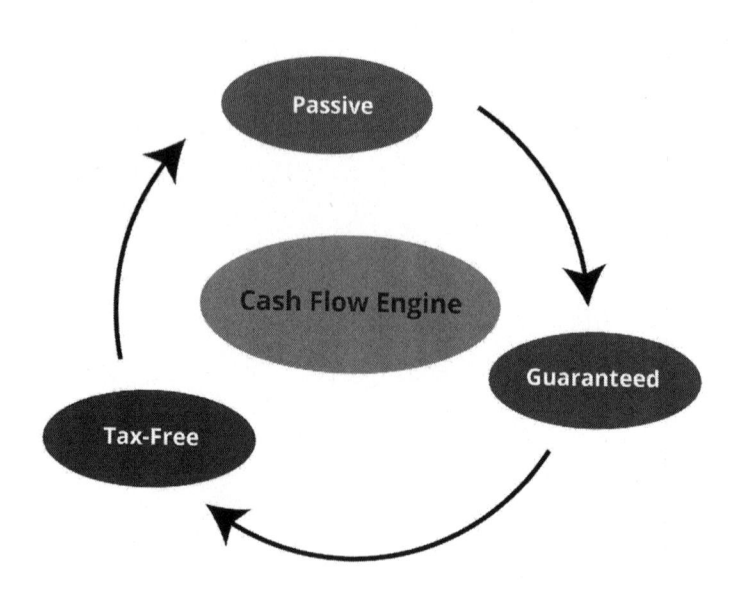

You Need the Right Strategy

I've written extensively about the symptoms of America's Retirement Income Crisis, but I've spoken very little about solutions.

It is extremely important that you use financial tools that allow you to prepare for inflation, and to reduce, or even eliminate interest rates, as well as give you consistent cash flow in retirement.

There are proven strategies that can give you all of that, as well as remove tax and market risk. There are solutions out there, non-government dependent solutions, that can help solve the crisis.

In this book, I'm going to show you those solutions. I'm going to guide you down a path toward your ideal investment strategy.

Are you ready?

Chapter Seven:

Is There A Perfect Investment?

Will and Kae stared at each other from across the kitchen table. His brow was crinkled with worry and her eyes were damp.

They couldn't process the news. As hard as they tried, they couldn't believe what their accountant and financial planner had just told them.

Will, who was 55, was going to have to work for another 20 years.

His 401(k) hadn't recovered from the 2000 and 2008 market crashes as well as he had hoped. It had made up a lot of lost ground in the recent few years, but he was still nowhere near his goal. If he retired any sooner, he would have to greatly reduce his lifestyle.

And Kae couldn't help. She was a public high school principal and her pension barely covered half of the bare minimum needed to get by. She contributed to her 503(b), but similar to Will, her accounts hadn't fully recovered from the most recent market crashes either. She didn't have enough saved to cover Will and speed up his retirement.

"What am I going to do, Kae?" Will asked, his jaw tense.

"Why don't we try calling that number we heard on the radio? You know? The one about alternative retirement strategies."

"Do you really think they're going to be able to help?" Will asked.

"It's worth a shot," Kae replied.

Reluctantly, Will nodded his head. He really didn't want to work for another 20 years...

A few days later, they walked into Gene's office, an agent with the Heydari Wealth Group. They sat down and quickly divulged their financial concerns.

"What are your goals?" Gene asked, smiling.

"I want to retire in 10 years, not 20. Is that even possible?" Will asked, doubt in his voice.

"It might be," Gene replied.

"Your radio ad mentioned some alternative strategies..." Kae said, her voice trailing off.

"Yes, and one of them may be right for you," Gene said, "but before we talk about possible solutions, let me be upfront. There is no perfect asset or financial strategy. Each one has pros and cons. However, some have better features than others. Let's determine your ideal investment strategy."

"Oh!" Kae exclaimed. "I like this!"

Gene laughed, "Good. Tell me, what's the first quality your ideal investment should have?"

"I want my money accessible," Will said, quickly.

#1) Accessibility

Kae's eyes lit up. "Yes! Accessibility would be great!"

Will nodded. "Just last year, Kae's brother had a real estate investment opportunity that we had to pass on."

Kae shook her head, her voice angry. "It made me so mad! We had enough cash in Will's 401(k) but couldn't access it without paying crazy fees! It's Will's money! He should be able to access it!"

Gene nodded, "Yes, that's very frustrating."

"And, what if there's an emergency?" Will asked. "My mom's health has been slowly getting worse. What if I need to access my money to pay for her care? I'll have no choice but to pay the fees."

"Accessibility is very important," Gene said. "What else?"

"Well, we're here because of the market," said Kae, rolling her eyes. "How about a strategy without any risk?"

#2) Minimal to No Risk

"So, if I could show you an asset with ABSOLUTELY no risk, no credit risk, default risk, interest rate risk, market risk, lawsuit risk, etc., that be attractive to you?"

"Yes, of course," Will and Kae said, almost in unison.

"I hate to be the bearer of bad news, but before we go any further, every investment comes with a little bit of risk. The only investments the government considers 'safe' are investments made with the bank. Those investments are backed by the FDIC - the Federal Deposit Insurance Corporation."

"But some banks were among the companies that went bankrupt in 2008! That doesn't make any sense!" Kae said, her fists clenched on her lap."

"No, it doesn't," Gene said. "Nothing is really risk-*free*, but there *are* a few strategies that will come pretty close."

"Great," said Will.

"What else are you looking for?" asked Gene.

"Hmm," said Will, "how about a strategy without any fees?"

#3) No Fees

Gene leaned back in his chair.

"Your perfect investment strategy is free?" He asked.

"Yes, of course," Will said. "Who wants to pay fees?"

"Let me ask you this," Gene said. "If you need heart surgery, do you expect your cardiologist to do it for free?"

"No, that would be silly," Kae said.

"Do you ask your doctor how much money he or she will make on the surgery?"

"No," Will said, shifting his weight from side to side in his chair.

"So, why should your investment strategy be free? First and foremost, you need a strategy that accomplishes your goals, right?" Gene asked, leaning forward.

Will and Kae nodded.

"We want to know and understand the fees, sure, but ultimately, because this is long-term investment planning, we're looking for the best strategy. The focus should be on your main goals and objectives, not just to eliminate fees.

"Yes, there are strategies out there that have high fees and low accessibility in the beginning, but we're talking about long-term investing, right? In the long-run, if that strategy can help you accomplish your goals and generate consistent retirement cashflow, aren't the fees worth it?

Will and Kae looked at Gene, unresponsive.

"Ok, think about it like this," Gene continued. "Do you own a house?"

"Yes, we just paid off a 30-year mortgage," Will said as Kae nodded.

"Did you know that first 10 years, most Americans pay 80% in interest charges?" Gene asked.

"Yes, I think I heard something like that," said Will.

"Why do you think most Americans are willing to pay that much in interest for 10 years?"

"Because they want a house!" said Kae.

"Exactly," said Gene. "If your goal is to buy a house, and the only way to do that is to mortgage the purchase, you have to be willing to pay a majority of the interest up front. In my opinion, the same concept should be applied to your financial goals."

"Ok, that makes sense," Kae said.

"I just thought of something else our investment strategy needs," said Will. "We need an unlimited Rate of Return."

#4) Unlimited ROR

"Yes, we definitely do," said Kae. "We need to make up for those losses in 2008."

"You want unlimited upside? You want an unlimited ROR?" Gene asks.

"That certainly would be nice," said Will. "But that's what the stock market promises, right?"

"Yes, typically when you invest in the market, the sky's the limit. But that isn't the only strategy that allows for unlimited growth."

"Oh really?" Kae asked, leaning forward.

"Really," said Gene, smiling. There are strategies the wealthy have been using for decades that feature an unlimited ROR. These strategies aren't advertised, which is probably why you haven't heard of them."

"Why aren't they being advertised?" Asked Will.

"That's a good question and I'll tell you my theory. But first, I want to make sure I understand everything you're looking for in your ideal investment strategy. Anything else?"

Will and Kae looked at each other and shrugged their shoulders.

"We can't think of anything," said Kae.

"What about a strategy that is 100% tax efficient? How does that sound?" Gene asked.

#5) 100% Tax Efficient

"What does that even mean?" asked Will.

"If the investment is 100% tax efficient, the money going in is tax-deferred, grows tax-free, is withdrawn tax-free, and is passed on to your heirs, tax-free," replied Gene.

"OK, well that isn't even possible," said Kae, as she sits back in her chair.

Gene laughed and said, "You're right. Nothing goes in tax-free and nothing comes out tax-free. Somewhere along the way, you have to pay taxes."

Will nodded his head and sat back in his chair.

"Let's make sure I've got this straight," Gene said and pushed back from his desk.

He walked over to the whiteboard in his office and wrote down the following list:

Ideal Investment Strategy

1. Accessibility
2. Zero Risk
3. No Fees
4. Unlimited ROR
5. 100% Tax Efficient

As soon as he was done writing, Kae said, "Sign me up!"

The ASERT Test

Kae sat back in her chair.

"You're kidding, right Kae? You know something like that doesn't exist," said Will.

"Yes, of course, Will," Kae said and rolled her eyes.

"No, the perfect strategy doesn't exist, which is probably why you're here, right?"

The coupled nodded.

"While there isn't a *perfect* strategy out there, depending on your individual goals and needs, some strategies are better than others. Nothing is perfect, right? So, doesn't it make sense to pick the strategy that *best* satisfies your combined objectives? Doesn't it make sense to pick the strategy that best satisfies your need for accessibility, safety, a high rate of return, tax efficiency, and low costs?

Think about the assets you currently have in your portfolio. Are any of them accessible? Are any of them safe from risk? How much are you paying in fees and what kind of ROR are you getting? And what about tax liability? Are you tax diversified?"

Will stared up at the ceiling and reviewed his assets in his head while Kay looked down and started counting on her fingers.

"I'll make this simple," Gene said. "At Heydari Wealth Group, we use the **ASERT** test to determine how different financial strategies stack up against your ideal investment strategy."

"The educator in me loves acronyms. What does that stand for?" Kae asks.

"Accessibility, Safety, Expense, Returns, and Taxability."

Pros and Cons to Every Strategy

"There are pros and cons to every investment strategy," Gene continued. "There are some assets that don't offer any accessibility and others that cost too much. For example, the stock market is accessible and has an unlimited ROR, but it's risky.

"Take a look at this chart. It lists the most common strategies, and their LISERT scores."

He turned his computer around and showed Will and Kae the following chart:

Strategy	Accessible	Safety	Expense	Returns	Taxability
IRA	No	no	no	yes	tax deferral
401K	No	no	no	yes	tax deferral
Pension	No	yes	no	yes	tax deferral
CD	Yes	yes	yes	no	taxable
Roth IRA	No	no	no	yes	tax advantage
Stock Market	Yes	no	yes	yes	taxable

The couple studied the screen for several moments.

"It's my job to help determine the best asset based on your objectives and goals," Gene said. "Throughout my career, I have seen many, many clients search long and hard for that perfect investment strategy.

"Guess what? They never found it! And the worst part? In the process, they lost years and years of compounding interest."

"That's a shame," Kae said and nodded.

"If I can find that asset for you, an asset that fits your goals and objectives, would you consider including it in your current investment portfolio?"

"Yes, we would certainly consider it," Kae said.

"Great. Before I tell you about my favorite strategy, a strategy that many of my clients have used to triple and quadruple their wealth, let's talk about some other alternative solutions."

Chapter Eight:

What Do You Know About These Popular Private Wealth Strategies?

Before we continue with our story, and I tell you how many of my clients have been able to maximize their wealth, I first want to take a moment to talk to you about some popular alternative strategies, gold, hard money lending, and income properties.

There's Gold in These Hills!

Like I mentioned at the beginning of this chapter, I believe in a diverse portfolio...and I'm not alone.

That's why many people, all around the world, invest in gold.

Do you invest in **gold**? Do you know someone who does?

I used to be fascinated with gold. From 2010 to 2014, I watched a TV show called *Gold Rush* on the Discovery Channel.

The show is still on today and follows different family-run mining companies, primarily in Alaska[42] (about 400 miles northeast of Anchorage, Alaska).

The family-run businesses focused on placer gold mining, or the mining of stream bed deposits for minerals. This type of mining is done by open-pit mining, surface level excavation, or tunneling.[43]

Every week, I would watch as the miners literally dug for gold. It was fascinating.

And as a bonus, the show would constantly update me on the price of gold. It was great[44].)

Why Gold?

A lot of people invest in gold because they believe it will hold its value. It's a tangible commodity. An ounce of gold will forever be an ounce of gold, right? People associate precious metals with stability. They believe it will protect them if the economy tanks. Gold is conservative.

There are other benefits of gold, too. It's accessible in that you don't have to call your broker or 401(k) account manager. You can take your ounce of gold to a precious metal trader in your hometown and sell it for cold, hard cash.

You may even be able to find a trader at the mall!

Are You A Doomsday Prepper?

Buying gold was very popular in 2008, after the market crash...and based on the increased level of commercials I've seen and heard recently, it seems to be making a comeback.

You may not know the commercials I'm talking about, but they're very popular. One of them goes a little something like this:

> "The US National Debt is at an all-time high and growing by $7 billion per day. It's only a matter of time before this whole thing implodes. And when it does, our country is going to be in a situation that it has never experienced before. You better make sure that you own gold coins to protect yourself for when this time comes. If you invest in stocks and bonds, then your fortunes are tied to how good or bad the economy is doing. BUT, if you invest in gold, you can insulate your wealth from economic turmoil. You need hard assets like gold so that you can truly protect your wealth[45]."

Let's break this commercial down. What is it really saying?

The commercial is telling us to invest in gold because the economy is probably going to "implode". It is agitating our fears about the future of our economy and our wealth and providing us with a "hard asset" solution like precious metals. The idea is that when all everything else fails, gold will hold its value.

But I'm not convinced that it will.

Take a look at the following chart.

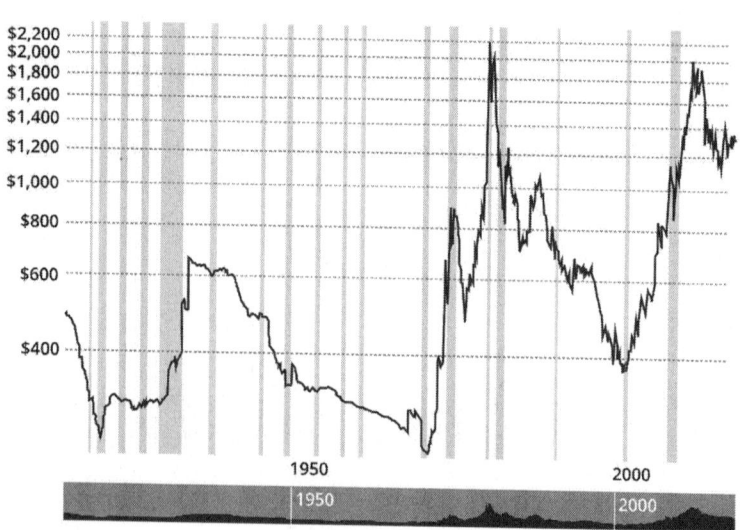

Price of Gold

As you can see, the price of gold fluctuates, just like the stock market. In February of 1980, gold hit its peak and sold for $2,109.45 an ounce, but it wasn't until February of 2012 22-years later that gold came close to that number again, selling for $1,978.77 an ounce[46]. At the end of 2017, it was selling for $1,302.66 an ounce. Gold is subjected to volatility, just like the market.

So, will gold hold its value? We really don't know, do we?

The question I always ask my clients is:

If the economy <u>never</u> implodes, would you still want to keep a major of portion of your wealth in gold?

Almost everyone I talk to says, "No."

Gold Provides No Cash Flow Until It's Sold

Gold gives you absolutely no cash flow. It doesn't earn any dividends or interest on its own. You have to sell it in order to support your lifestyle.

It might make sense to hold a small amount of gold, <u>in case</u> the world goes to hell in a hand basket, but I wouldn't recommend investing *all* of your wealth in precious metals.

Executive Order 6102

For argument's sake, let's say gold *does* retain its value. If the economy really implodes, if the government is forced to start repaying their debt, do you really think your gold is safe?

The U.S. Government has a history of confiscating gold.

On April 5, 1933, President Franklin D. Roosevelt signed Executive Order 6102, "forbidding the hoarding of gold coin, gold bullion, and gold certificates within the continental United States".

POSTMASTER: PLEASE POST IN A CONSPICUOUS PLACE.—JAMES A. FARLEY, Postmaster General

UNDER EXECUTIVE ORDER OF THE PRESIDENT

issued April 5, 1933

all persons are required to deliver

ON OR BEFORE MAY 1, 1933

all **GOLD COIN, GOLD BULLION, AND GOLD CERTIFICATES** now owned by them to a Federal Reserve Bank, branch or agency, or to any member bank of the Federal Reserve System.

Executive Order

FORBIDDING THE HOARDING OF GOLD COIN, GOLD BULLION AND GOLD CERTIFICATES.

[body of executive order]

THE WHITE HOUSE
April 5, 1933

FRANKLIN D. ROOSEVELT

For Further Information Consult Your Local Bank

GOLD CERTIFICATES may be identified by the words "GOLD CERTIFICATE" appearing thereon. The serial number and the Treasury seal on the face of a GOLD CERTIFICATE are printed in YELLOW. Be careful not to confuse GOLD CERTIFICATES with other issues which are redeemable in gold but which are not GOLD CERTIFICATES. Federal Reserve Notes and United States Notes are "redeemable in gold" but are not "GOLD CERTIFICATES" and are not required to be surrendered

Special attention is directed to the exceptions allowed under Section 2 of the Executive Order

CRIMINAL PENALTIES FOR VIOLATION OF EXECUTIVE ORDER
$10,000 fine or 10 years imprisonment, or both, as provided in Section 9 of the order

Secretary of the Treasury.

The law required all Americans to surrender to the Federal Reserve all but a small amounts of gold coin, gold bullion, and gold certificates. In exchange, they were given $20.67 an ounce ($391 today). Failure to submit resulted in a fine of up to $10,000 (almost $190,000 today) and/or up to 10 years in prison.

At the time, after the Great Depression, the government needed gold to boost the economy and print more money...so they took it[47].

You may think that investing in gold is a way to protect your wealth against an unstable economic future, but do you really trust the government not to take yours if they need it?

When you think about it like that, when you know our government's history with gold, it suddenly feels like a riskier investment, right?

And as we know from the chart we studied earlier, gold fluctuates in price. How can we trust that it will hold its value?

	Quick Buying Guide - Gold
Pros	Holds its value (maybe) No fees Accessible (only if you sell it)
Cons	Price fluctuates like the market The government has a history of confiscating gold Growth is taxable

Hard Money Lending

Enough about gold.

Another alternative wealth and retirement building strategy is **hard money lending.**

This is a very popular strategy that has the potential to make you a lot of money.

If you have enough capital, you can loan money to business owners privately. The benefit for them is they don't have to go through the qualification process with a bank. The benefit for you is that you earn interest on the loan.

And the best part? You can use their business as collateral.

Let me give you an example:

John is a business owner and he needs a million dollars.

We loan him the million dollars, charge him 12% interest, and use his business property, valued at $1.5 million, as collateral.

Regardless of whether or not he repays, the return is predictable. Either we receive the 12% return we set up or, if he doesn't repay his loan, just like a bank, we can take over his property.

Hard Money Lending is a great strategy because you have complete control over the loan. You choose the borrower and decide which rates you're going to charge them.

And these are short-term loans; a one to two-year commitment, max.

Those are the positives...but like with just about everything, there are negatives, too.

First of all, hard money lending is complicated and the laws governing the practice vary by state. Make sure you understand what you can and cannot do. Before you decide to implement the strategy, make sure you have thoroughly done your research.

This strategy can also be risky. There are many hard money lending companies out there taking advantage of investors' money and committing fraud. If you do this, make sure your name is on the title and deed of trust.

Another risk is that the business owner defaults on the loan. Sure, you're getting the property, but the foreclosure process could take years, years your money isn't earning interest.

Finally, there's the risk of another real estate crash. If that happens, suddenly the value of the property isn't worth as much. If you lend out too much money to the person and if the property crashes in value now you're in the negative, so you're not going to get all your money back.

If you have the capital, hard money lending can be very lucrative, but it has its own set of risks, just like everything else.

Quick Buying Guide: Hard Money Lending	
Pros	Predictable return Complete control over loan Short-term loans
Cons	Laws vary state by state Easily susceptible to fraud Long foreclosure process Real estate market could crash Returns are taxable

How Much Do You Know About Income Properties?

Earlier in the book we talked about 3 types of cash flow:

1. Passive Cash Flow
2. Guaranteed Cash Flow
3. Tax-Free Cash Flow

In the upcoming chapters, we're going to talk about how to generate Guaranteed and Tax-Free Cash Flow, but first I want to focus on Passive Cash Flow (PCF).

One of the best ways to generate PCF is by investing in **income properties**. For decades, this strategy has been a part of many American millionaires' financial plans because real estate is one of the most effective wealth building vehicles. It is an important component of a well-diversified portfolio. Income properties can be a valuable addition to your portfolio and can provide income right now. It can also serve as an asset you build for your retirement.

There are a ton of benefits to having income properties, but like any other strategy, there are also some downsides. If done correctly, they can provide a steady passive income, help reduce taxes, and build something for the future.

Recurring Income, Growth Over Time, and Tax Deductions, Oh My!

Investing in income properties can provide steady income. Buy it, fix it up, and rent it out.

And while you're renting it, the property appreciated, and you build equity. It really is win-win.

But that's not all.

In addition to steady income and growth, there are tax benefits. You can deduct most rental expenses like property taxes, repair and maintenance expenses, insurance expenses, professional services, and travel expenses.

<u>On top of all those deductions, the government also allows you to depreciate the purchase price of your property based on a set depreciation schedule, even if your property is actually *appreciating* in value.</u>

I know that doesn't sound right...but even though your property is appreciating in value, in the eyes of

IRS, the value of the building is *depreciating*, so they allow you to write that off every year based on a set depreciation schedule.

It's All About Diversification

We talked earlier about not putting all of your money in one basket...

The same goes for rental properties. If you're going to go that route, don't invest everything you have into one rental property. It's important to spread your money out across multiple properties, especially if you're going to buy those properties out of state.

Why?

If you have multiple properties and one of your tenants moves out, your passive income won't be affected as dramatically. Plus, we typically have to mortgage these properties, meaning there's a monthly payment to the bank that needs to be covered. If you only have one property, when the tenant moves out, you don't have a lot of financial leeway.

Can You Manage My Property?

Although rental properties can certainly generate sizable income, it's important to remember that owning and managing a property is still a job. Unless you want to do this as a hobby, and if you are as busy as most of the people I talk to, it might make sense to hire a **property management company**.

Management companies deal directly with applicants and tenants, saving you time.

You also don't have to worry about anything. They will market the property, collect the rent, handle maintenance and repairs, and even pursue evictions.

It's important to do your due diligence when you hire a property management company. A good management company brings its know-how and experience to your property, giving you piece of mind knowing your property is in good hands.

If you're interested in learning more about how to benefit from income properties, visit www.TheRetirementEpidemic.com to schedule a complimentary consultation.

Real estate isn't for everyone, but when I sit down with you, we will take a look at your portfolio and see if it makes sense to diversify a portion of your portfolio into a passive cash flow vehicle like income properties.

If it does, when combined with another strategy I'm going to tell you about a little later, income properties have the potential to grow your wealth much faster.

	Quick Buying Guide: Income Properties
Pros	Generates Passive Cash-Flow Asset Grows in Value Over Time Property and Related Expenses are Tax Deductions
Cons	Mortgage Payments No Control When Tenant Leaves Property Management Lack of Liquidity Tax Benefits May Change in the Future You Need to Qualify

How Do These Alternative Strategies Stack Up?

So, what happens when we compare these alternative strategies to our ideal investment strategy?

Let's apply the ASERT test and take a look.

Strategy	Accessibility	Safety	Expense	Returns	Taxability
IRA	no	no	No	yes	tax deferral
401K	no	no	No	yes	tax deferral
Pension	no	yes	No	yes	tax deferral
CD	yes	yes	Yes	no	taxable
Roth IRA	no	no	No	yes	tax advantage
Stock Market	yes	no	Yes	yes	taxable
Precious Metals	yes	no	Yes	NA	taxable
Hard Money Lending	no	yes	No	yes	taxable
Income Properties	no	yes	Yes	yes	taxable

Each of these strategies has pros and cons, and depending on your unique situation, some may be better for you than others.

The idea here is to diversify. Remember, don't put your financial eggs all in one basket.

For some, it might make sense to have 10% of their portfolio invested in precious metals or use hard money lending for a short-term, high-interest investment.

It might make sense for others to benefit from income properties.

Regardless of the specific tools you chose to use, your investment strategy should match your retirement needs. That's what's important.

I know you're excited to get back to our story. I am, too.

But first I want to talk to you about something serious. Some of us are facing a **Retirement Income Gap**.

What am I talking about?

Turn the page to find out.

Chapter Nine:

Curing the Retirement Income Gap

In Southern California, in the San Gabriel Mountains, there is a **Bridge to Nowhere**. It was built in 1936 and was meant to be connected to a road that spanned from the San Gabriel Valley to the small town of Wrightwood, located 77 miles northeast of L.A.[48]

The bridge was built, but the project was never completed.

Halfway through construction, the region was hit with the Los Angeles flood of 1938, one of the biggest floods in the area's history. It was caused when two massive Pacific storms dumped almost a year's worth of water on Los Angeles, Orange, and Riverside counties... in just a few days.

The flood caused $78 million in damage, equivalent to about $1.36 billion today[49], and washed the construction site away, leaving the bridge stranded.

The Bridge to Nowhere still stands today, accessible via a 10-mile roundtrip hike.

The Retirement Income Gap

Why am I talking about a bridge stranded in the middle of the Southern Californian wilderness?

The bridge was meant to be part of a road connecting two larger roads. But, because construction was never completed, instead of roads, there are large gaps.

Like the gaps in that road, many Americans will also see gaps in their retirement income. I'm talking about the **Retirement Income Gap**.

In the last chapter, we talked about Passive Cash Flow and rental properties.

When thinking about retirement income, there really are two categories: guaranteed and non-guaranteed. In retirement, we want to focus on Guaranteed Cash Flow.

Throughout this book, we've talked about the Retirement Epidemic, and how millions of Americans don't have enough saved for retirement. This disease festers and spreads when it comes to guaranteed income in retirement.

Non-guaranteed income is income you cannot set in stone. The amount you receive varies year to year (or in some cases, month to month) because it's based on investment performance. Typically, these accounts are tied to the market. Income you receive from 401(k)s, IRAs, and stocks is non-guaranteed income.

On the other hand, guaranteed income is money you can count on, year after year, month after month. It's income you cannot outlive. Some people refer to this as **longevity insurance** because you are protected against the possibility of outliving your financial resources. Examples of guaranteed income are Social Security, pensions, and annuities.

Do You Know Your Guaranteed Retirement Income Gap?

When planning for retirement, you really need to think about your **Guaranteed Income Gap (GIG)**, or the gap between your guaranteed and non-guaranteed income.

Do you have a GIG? Do you know?

Whenever I sit down with my clients, that's the first thing we figure out.

We start out by using a Social Security Maximizer to ensure we take full advantage of this guaranteed income benefit. This step, in and of itself is very important. Many people don't know how to properly complete a social security report and end up losing a lot of money they're legally entitled to.

If the client has a pension (another guaranteed income tool), we take a look at those numbers next. But if you can remember from earlier in the book, most Americans <u>don't</u> have pensions anymore. It's a retirement planning tool that has almost gone extinct.

Finally, we look at how much income the client expects to need in retirement, both monthly and annually. The difference between this number, and the social security and pension payments, is the client's guaranteed income gap.

How Many Americans Have a GIG?

Earlier in the book we talked about the 6 symptoms of America's retirement income crisis. (If you haven't read that yet, you should. You can find the information in Chapter Two.)

Retirement Savings Have Stagnated in the New Millennium
Mean retirement account savings of families by age, 1989-2013 (2013 dollars)

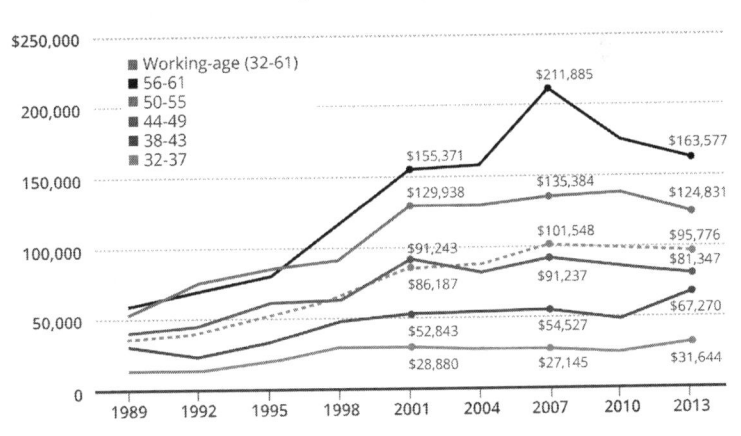

Legend:
- Working-age (32-61)
- 56-61
- 50-55
- 44-49
- 38-43
- 32-37

Selected data points:
- $211,885 (2007 peak)
- $163,577 (2013)
- $155,371 (2001)
- $135,384 (2007)
- $129,938 (2001)
- $124,831 (2013)
- $101,548 (2007)
- $95,776 (2013)
- $91,243 (2001)
- $91,237 (2007)
- $86,187 (2001)
- $81,347 (2013)
- $67,270 (2013)
- $52,843 (2001)
- $54,527 (2007)
- $28,880 (2001)
- $27,145 (2007)
- $31,644 (2013)

Years: 1989, 1992, 1995, 1998, 2001, 2004, 2007, 2010, 2013

Note: Retirement account savings include 401(k)s, IRAs, and Keogh plans.
Source: EPI analysis of Survey of Consumer Finance data, 2013.

We know that mean retirement savings, per household, is low. Per the chart below, it looks like most Americans still haven't recovered from the 2008 market crash.

And when we break it down by age group, the numbers get even more shocking.

Most Families - Even Those Approaching Retirement - Have Little or No Retirement Savings
Mean retirement account savings of families by age, 1989-2013 (2013 dollars)

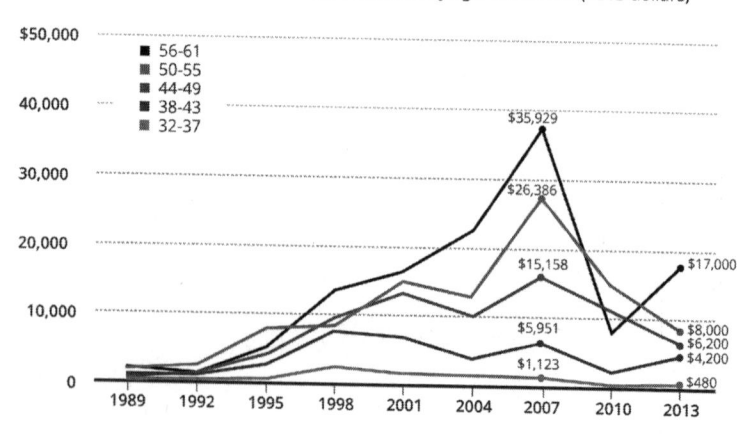

- 56-61
- 50-55
- 44-49
- 38-43
- 32-37

2007 values: $35,929; $26,386; $15,158; $5,951; $1,123
2013 values: $17,000; $8,000; $6,200; $4,200; $480

Note: Scale changed for visibility. Retirement account savings include 401(k)s, IRAs, and Keogh plans.
Source: EPI analysis of Survey of Consumer Finance data, 2013.

When we think about these preexisting shortfalls, and combine them with longer lifespans, the results are potentially disastrous.

Just how disastrous?

Over 30 million Americans have a guaranteed income gap[50].

According to a 2016 Consumer Expenditure Survey for the U.S. Bureau of Labor Statistics, Americans 65 and over on average receive $2,000 a month from their pensions and social security but spend an average of $2,600 a month on housing, healthcare, utilities, and food. That's a $600 GIG that needs to be covered[51].

How Much of Your Retirement Savings Should Be Guaranteed?

No one really talks about the guaranteed income gap… or makes plans to do anything about it.

It's like that sad, lonely Bridge to Nowhere.

Why?

Because there really are only a few strategies that can do that. (There *is* one option I will touch on in a bit.)

"That's what the money in my 401(k) or IRA is for. The money in those accounts will cover my Retirement Income Gap."

But if you remember, money in these types of accounts isn't guaranteed. Those returns depend on the performance of those investments because the money is typically tied to the market. Periodic market set-backs are easy to shrug off when you're in your 20s, 30s, or even 40s, because you still have time to recover.

But as we get older, it becomes more important to protect your money because it can take a very long time to recover.

Just how long?

The Amount that Must be Re-Earned to Fully Recover from a Stock Market Loss

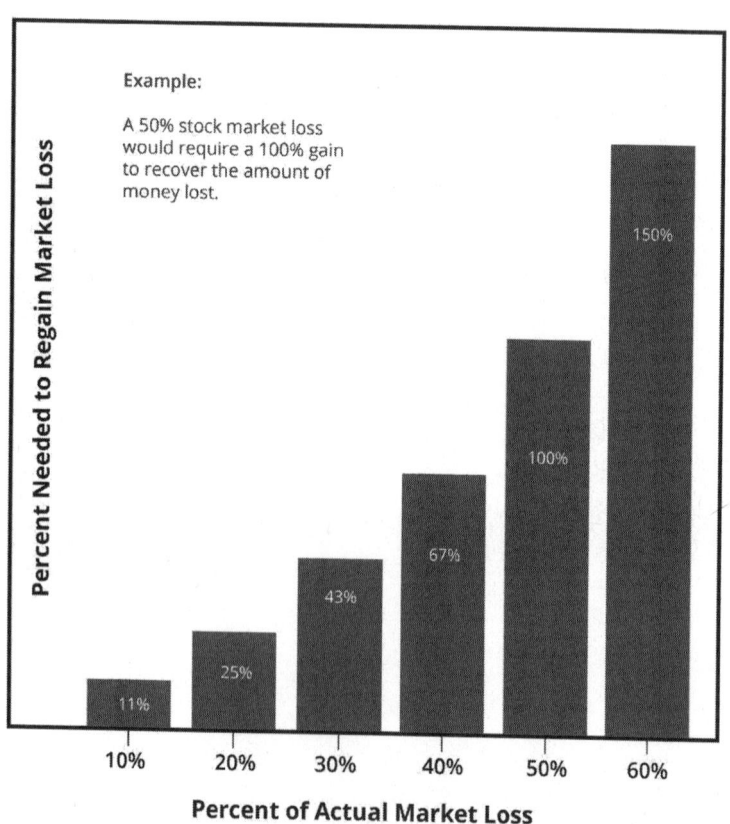

Example:

A 50% stock market loss would require a 100% gain to recover the amount of money lost.

Percent of Actual Market Loss	Percent Needed to Regain Market Loss
10%	11%
20%	25%
30%	43%
40%	67%
50%	100%
60%	150%

Portfolio Loss	Gain Needed to Restore Loss	1 Year	2 Year	3 Year	4 Year	5 Year	10 Year
-10.0%	-11.1%	25.5%	74.4%	81.6%	78.4%	77.8%	93.5%
-20.0%	-25.0%	25.0%	48.7%	68.4%	67.6%	72.2%	93.5%
-35.0%	-54.0%	0.0%	17.9%	34.2%	56.8%	61.1%	93.5%
-50.0%	-100.0%	0.0%	0.0%	7.9%	13.5%	36.1%	80.6%
-65.0%	-186.0%	0.0%	0.0%	0.0%	2.7%	5.6%	61.3%

Percentage chance of recovery from loss within...

SOURCE: "The Match of Gains and Losses," Craig L. Israelsen, Ph. D., Woodbury School of Business, Utah Valley University, 2010.

To refresh your memory (we originally discussed this concept in Chapter Four), these two charts show how long it takes to recover from a market loss:

Still think you can count on your nonguaranteed income to fill your retirement income gap?

How Much Should You Have in Guaranteed Accounts?

Throughout this book, I have pointed out the risks of market-based investments for retirement. It takes too long to recover from market losses, time you don't have.

That's why it's vitally important to look at your GIG and reallocate a portion of your portfolio into guaranteed income products.

But how do you figure that out? How do you determine what percentage of your portfolio should be in guaranteed income products?

The Rule of 100

The Rule of 100 is going to help us figure out our specific GIG. It's simply an asset allocation and here's how it works.

> 100 - Your Age =
> Recommended Percentage of Portfolio
> Invested in Non-Guaranteed Funds (Equities)

The percentage of money in your non-guaranteed income accounts should be 100 minus your current age. If you are 60, for example, you should have 40% in nonguaranteed income (stocks) and 60% in guaranteed income.

There are two sources of guaranteed income I touched on at the beginning of this chapter: social security and pensions.

> ### #1: Social Security
>
> An aging population means the social security benefit fund is shrinking...rapidly.
>
> Starting in 2035, the Social Security Administration website states that the government will only be able to pay 75% of social security benefits.
>
> "Currently, the Social Security Board of Trustees projects program cost to rise by 2035 so that taxes will be enough to pay for only 75 percent of scheduled benefits."

Unless major changes are made before 2037, the government is scheduled to reduce social security payments by 24%. In 17 short years, the $1,368/month you receive in social security benefits is scheduled to drop to $1026.

In 1942, when social security was first established as a benefit, 42 people contributed to for every single person who received the benefit. In 2013, only 2.9 people contributed for every single person who received the benefit[2].

On top of that, as we've discussed time and time again, people are living much longer. In 1965, the average life expectancy for males was 64[52], and in 2017 it was 79[53].

All of these factors contribute to social security quickly running out of money.

#2: Pensions

Like we covered in chapter three, pensions (a.k.a. defined benefit plans) provide guaranteed income for life and are typically managed by the employer.

This used to be the way most Americans planned for retirement.

But in 1979, just under 70% of private sector working Americans relied on a pension to retire, compared to only about 13% today.

Most of us don't have pensions.

Top: Defined Benefit Plan (pension) vs Bottom: Defined Contribution Plan (401(k))

What Are Our Options?

Our guaranteed retirement income options are either shrinking or disappearing completely.

It seems like we're all out of options...

There is one more option that many of you have heard of and that many of you dislike.

I'm talking about **annuities**, the retirement tool everyone loves to hate.

Back in 2009, when I started working in this field, I had the same feeling about annuities as most of the people I talk to today.

I didn't like annuities. In fact, I hated them.

One night, I was watching a special program on TV; they were running a sting operation on financial advisors. Specifically, they were focusing on life insurance agents who pitched annuities to seniors.

I watched as these crooked insurance agents used every sales tactic imaginable to try and generate a sale and "make a big fat commission". I watched them withhold certain truths to make the sale.

I don't have a problem with people earning commissions for a living, but I *do* have a problem with agents who put their personal interests before the client.

As you can imagine, at this point I had a very bad taste in my mouth about annuities. All I'd seen and heard was negative.

And there are still a lot of negatives about annuities circulating the newsfeeds today. If you do a quick Google search, all you'll find will be negatives about annuities.

"10 Reasons Not to Buy Annuities"

"Annuities Are Too Expensive"

"Insurance Agents Makes Too Much in Commission"

"Insurance Company Keeps Your Money If You Die"

With search results like that, why would anyone put their hard-earned money into one of these products?

Or better yet, why are we even talking about annuities?

Well, let's fast forward a few years:

After a few years in the business and as my practice grew, a lot of my clients started asking me about annuities.

I used to always refer them to a colleague of mine, but then other financial advisors started telling me not all annuities are bad. So, I decided to spend some time to do my due diligence and study annuities.

And what I found was shocking.

Annuities Have Changed

When I did my research, I found that a lot of the negatives I had heard about annuities had to do with the risk and cost of **variable annuities**.

Variable annuities are risky because they expose your money to the stock market; they basically buy stocks and mutual funds and hold them inside an insurance wrapper.

And their fee structure is like the fee structure for mutual funds. Once you add up all the fees, it can get very expensive.

But today, there are new types of annuities being offered. The one in particular that caught my eye while I was researching was a **Fixed Indexed Annuity (FIA)**.

Why?

It offers what my clients are looking for.

Basically, a FIA is a contract between you and an insurance company that guarantees some type of payment.

Unlike variable annuities, an FIA (or as we in the business like to call them, a hybrid annuity) is not invested in the stock market. If the market crashes, you don't lose anything. Not only is your principal always protected, you also have the potential to earn interest when the market goes up. You can lock in your gains during good years without having to worry about losing anything in down years.

Plus, the fee structure is much more forgiving. If there are any fees, they are limited.

There are two types of FIA: guaranteed lifetime income or consistent growth.

There Are Two Types of FIAs:

#1 Provide Lifetime Income:

This type of FIA provides lifetime income that you cannot outlive. You also you have the potential to choose the Index Earning Income. This allows you increase your payments annually to keep up with inflation.

#2 Provide Protection and Consistent Growth Over Time:

This type of FIA provides consistent growth, very minimal fees if any fees at all, and provides more options as times moves forward.

Is an Annuity Right for You?

It could be.

After we sit down with our clients and determine their GIG, we can decide whether or not an annuity is right for you, and if it is, which FIA makes the most sense.

About five years ago, I met with my client, Tom, who is 65.

Almost all of his investments were in the market, and his main concern was losing everything if the market crashed, like it did in 2008. He had lost just over 40% of his portfolio and as of 2013, still hadn't recovered.

According to the Rule of 100, he should have 65% of his money in guaranteed income accounts and 35% in nonguaranteed accounts (100-65=35).

When Tom came to see me, he was planning on retiring soon, so it made sense to go with the first type of FIA, the one that guarantees income for life.

If you're thinking about an annuity to help close your Guaranteed Retirement Income Gap, be careful. There are still a lot of "bad" annuities out there...and a lot of agents trying to sell them.

Before you purchase an FIA, make sure it has a majority of these items:

1) 100% Principal Protection

2) Rate of Return That Is Locked in Every Year

3) Guaranteed Lifetime Income

4) Annual Reset

5) Can Be Used with Qualified and Non-Qualified Funds

6) Little to No Fees

7) A+ Rated Insurance Company, 100+ Years in Existence

8) Index Options

9) No Confusing Algorithm, Easy to Understand

The guaranteed income gap is very real and very scary. Instead of a Bridge to Nowhere, many Americans will have a Retirement to Nowhere, and will be left with more expenses than they have the money to pay for.

Americans used to have more options...but social security is dwindling, and pensions have all but disappeared.

Thankfully, the third option, annuities, have changed over the years. Today, Fixed Indexed Annuities are an excellent solution.

If an annuity sounds interesting, and you still have a lot of questions, my firm can help. Visit www.TheRetirementEpidemic.com to schedule a complimentary consultation.

Strategy	Accessibility	Safety	Expense	Returns	Taxability
IRA	No	no	no	yes	tax deferral
401K	No	no	no	yes	tax deferral
Pension	No	yes	no	yes	tax deferral
CD	Yes	yes	yes	no	taxable
Roth IRA	No	no	no	yes	tax advantage
Stock Market	Yes	no	yes	yes	taxable
Precious Metals	Yes	no	yes	NA	taxable
Hard Money Lending	No	yes	no	yes	taxable
Income Properties	No	yes	yes	yes	taxable
Annuities	**No**	**yes**	**yes**	**no**	**depends**

Let's check back in with Will, Kae, and Gene to find out more about a retirement strategy that passes the ASERT test with flying colors. It also provides tax-free cash flow...

Chapter Ten:

The Power of the Index

"Now that we've got those alternative strategies out of the way," Gene said, taking a sip of water, "let's dig into the good stuff, the strategies that have helped many Heydari Wealth Group clients grow their money much, much faster, without ever losing a dime."

"Sounds great!" exclaimed Kae as Will smiled.

"Can we agree that you would rather take advantage of volatility than get burned by it?"

"Yes," Will said as Kae squeezed his arm.

"And you want take advantage of low tax rates, so you don't get stuck potentially paying a lot more in retirement, right?" Gene asked, leaning forward.

"Absolutely," Kae said, her eyes gleaming.

"Then you should consider an indexing strategy."

"I've never heard of that," Will said and he crossed his arms in front of his chest.

"It's not a well-known strategy, but it has been used by the world's biggest companies for executive retirement compensation and by the world's biggest banks to protect their capital. It has been used by U.S. Presidents and business tycoons like Walt Disney and J.C. Penney."

"How does it work?" Kae asked, smiling.

"Your money is linked to an index, like the S&P 500, for example," replied Gene.

"Ok," said Will, still dubious.

"When the index goes up, so does your account value, usually as much as 11-14%." Will squinted his eyes, but before he could speak, Gene continued. "But an indexing strategy has a floor of zero, meaning you can't lose money in down years."

"What?" Will asked and leaned forward.

"It's true. You don't lose money when the market crashes."

"Hmm," Will said, placing his elbows on the table. He looked at Kae.

"This strategy usually comes with an 11-14% cap, so you can't take full advantage of the good years, but because you never lose money, when the market rebounds, you can take advantage and pick right back up where you left off. Over a 20-year period, even

The Power of the Index

with the caps, you'll see more growth with an indexing strategy than with a market strategy. Here, let me show you what I'm talking about."

Gene clicked a few buttons with his mouse and turned his monitor around to face Will and Kae.

"What I'm about to show you demonstrates the basic difference between an index strategy and a market strategy.

Again, I want to clarify that an index strategy does NOT put your money in the stock market. It only links to it using a popular index, like the S&P 500 Index. A stock market strategy puts your money directly into the market, meaning it can go up and it can go down.

"Let's say you begin with $10,000. In year one, the S&P grows 10%. The same thing happens in year two. Right now, you have $12,100 in either an index or market account." Gene pointed to the line on the graph.

Index Strategy vs. Market Strategy

■ Index Strategy
■ Market Strategy

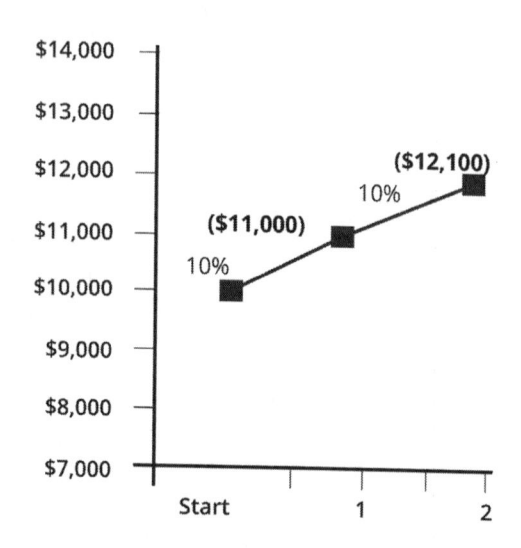

[Chart showing Index Strategy and Market Strategy from Start to Year 2. Start: $10,000. Year 1: $11,000 (10% increase). Year 2: $12,100 (10% increase).]

"Then, the market drops by 20%, and I think we all can agree that a 20% drop is possible, right?"

"Yes," said Kae, nodding.

"If you invested in the S&P, you would have $9,600 in your account after the 20% drop, but if your money was in an index strategy, you wouldn't lose anything, your account balance would remain $12,100."

Index Strategy vs. Market Strategy

```
Index Strategy
Market Strategy
```

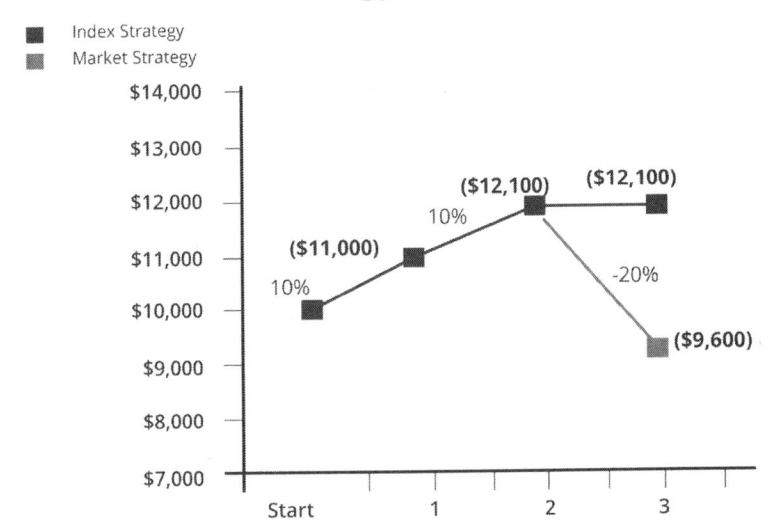

	Start	1	2	3
Market Strategy	$10,000	($11,000) 10%	($12,100) 10%	($9,600) -20%
Index Strategy			($12,100)	($12,100)

"Interesting," said Will, nodding.

"Let's say in year four the market drops another 17%. Now, your S&P account balance is down to approximately $7,900. How much do you think is in your index account?"

"$12,100?" Kae asks, unsure of her answer.

"That's exactly right," says Gene.

"Wow!" Kae almost shouts, very pleased with herself.

Index Strategy vs. Market Strategy

- Index Strategy
- Market Strategy

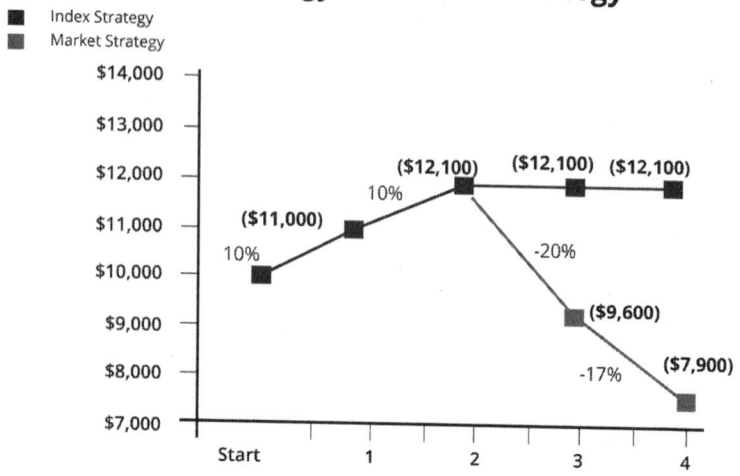

	Start	1	2	3	4
Index Strategy	$10,000	($11,000) 10%	($12,100) 10%	($12,100)	($12,100)
Market Strategy				($9,600) -20%	($7,900) -17%

"Right," said Gene. "There's a big difference between $12,100 and $7,900, especially when the market starts to rebound. In year five, the market makes a little comeback and the S&P increases by 15%.

"The market strategy, this line at the bottom of the graph, gets the full 15% return. That ends up being approximately $1,100, bringing your market account balance up to $9,100. The index strategy only gets a 12% increase, because it's capped, bumping its total value up to $13,550, another big difference."

Index Strategy vs. Market Strategy

■ Index Strategy
■ Market Strategy

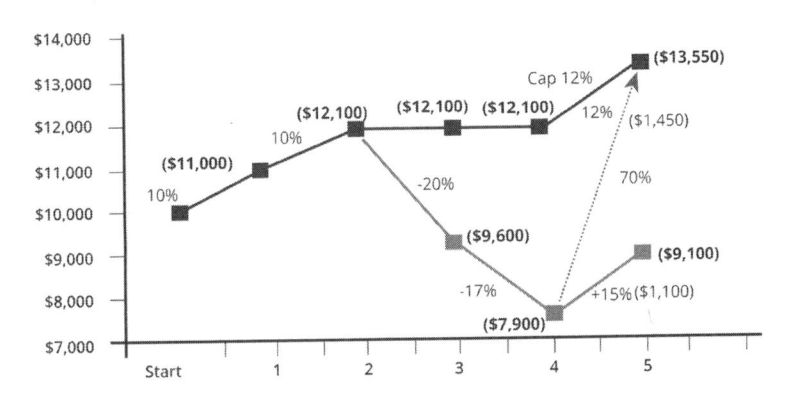

Point	Index Strategy	Market Strategy
Start	$10,000	$10,000
1	$11,000 (10%)	—
2	$12,100 (10%)	—
3	$12,100	$9,600 (-20%)
4	$12,100	$7,900 (-17%)
5	$13,550 (Cap 12%)	$9,100 (+15%) → $1,100 / $1,450 (70%)

"I really hate the cap," said Kae. "I hate the idea of missing out on gains."

"I understand," replied Gene. "That was hard for me to let go of, too. But take another look at this chart. In year four, the market strategy had $7,900 to the index strategy's $12,100. How much do you think the market has to grow in year five to make up for the losses in years three and four? How much does it have to grow to catch up to the index strategy?"

"Well, I have no idea," said Will.

"Isn't that your job?" Kae asked and then laughed.

"It *is* my job," Gene said and smiled. "The market has to grow by 70% to catch the index strategy."

"70%?" asked Kae, her eyebrows raised.

"That's right," Gene replied.

"Well, that's ridiculous," said Will as he pursed his lips.

"I would have to say I agree!" Kate exclaimed, clapping her hands.

"Do you now see why an indexing strategy is so powerful? Not only does it give you peace of mind because you know you're not going to lose your money when the market crashes, you never have to worry about 'catching up'. Plus, like I mentioned earlier, in the long run, your money is likely to see *more* growth. Let me use another example to prove it to you."

Which Strategy Do You Want Working for You?

"In the last example, I used hypothetical numbers," Gene continued. "Let's take a look at an historical example."

"That sounds great," said Will, smiling. He was starting to feel more hopeful. He didn't want to lose his money in the market again and was beginning to believe this index strategy could be the solution he had been looking for.

"I want you to look at one more chart," Gene said, flipping his monitor around. "This graph shows the history of three different investment strategies, from 1997 to 2017. Each account began with $100,000."

The Power of the Index

We Need A Strategy To Help Deal With Volatility

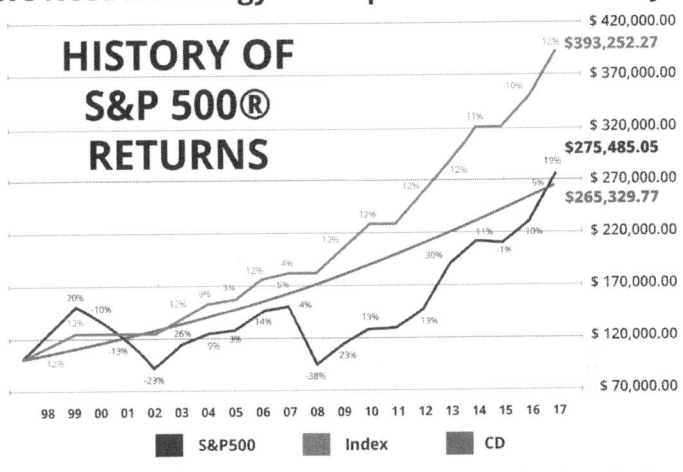

HISTORY OF S&P 500® RETURNS

	S&P500	Index	CD

Past performance is not a guarantee of future results. Investment will fluctuate and when redeemed may be worth more or less than when originally invested. S&P500 historical returns were source from http://en.wikipedia.org/wiki/S%26P_500_Index. The assumption of 12% cap is being applied to this hypothetical index scenario.

Gene sat back in his chair while Will and Kae looked at the graph.

"As you can see, over 20 years, a market strategy doesn't do too much better than a bank CD. All that stress earns you a whopping $10,155.28 (the difference between $275,485.05 and $265,329.77).

"But take a look at the index strategy. Because the index strategy never lost any money due to the stock market correction, it continued to grow right from where it left off. And even though the policy would have some fees like all assets or investments), the difference is still massive. You literally earn more ($117,766.50).

"This is an example of how we can use an indexing strategy to take advantage of market volatility. As you can see, after each market crash, there is typically a big rebound and several years of double-digit growth. Because you never lose money when the market crashes, when it rebounds and sees massive growth, you can capture the lion's share of that. In fact, the more the market swings back and forth, the more valuable this strategy becomes."

"Plus, we'll have that peace of mind we so desperately want," said Kae, as she squeezed Will's arm.

"Personally," said Gene and leaned forward, "I think an indexing strategy is a win-win."

The Pros and Cons of an Indexing Strategy

"Before I tell you the tool we use at the Heydari Wealth Group to harness that strategy, let me tell you some of the other benefits," said Gene.

"That sounds great," said Kae.

"An index strategy is also tax-advantaged."

"What does tax-advantaged really mean, anyway?" asked Will. "That's not the same as tax-deferred right?"

"No, not at all. Tax-advantaged means the money inside an index strategy grows tax-deferred and you can access it tax-free, unlike the money in brokerage or 401(k) accounts."

"Tax-free? Really" Will was definitely interested now.

"It works kind of like a Roth, where you pay taxes today and never have to worry about what tax rates are going to do in the future."

The Power of the Index

"Is there a limit to how much we can put in?" Kae asked.

"No, that's another benefit. Unlike a Roth, there are no limits," said Gene.

"Wonderful," said Kae as she leaned back in her chair.

"An index strategy also gives you flexibility and accessibility. There are some restrictions, but for the most part you can stop payments if you need to and access your cash at any time. Unlike a Roth, the money you have invested in an index strategy is accessible. You can gain access it whenever you need it."

"Sign me up," said Will.

"Yeah, no kidding," Kae said.

Gene laughed. "I'm glad to hear you're both excited about the strategy, but there are a few disadvantages, too, and I want to make sure you're aware of them before we move forward."

"I knew it was too good to be true," Will said as he crossed his arms and leaned back in his chair.

"There are disadvantages to every strategy, right?" Gene asked, never taking his eyes off Will. "For example, if you use a market strategy, the disadvantage is that your money is subject to market volatility. Sure, you can win big when the market is up, but when it crashes, you could lose almost everything."

"Exactly," said Kae smugly.

"Yes, I suppose you're right," said Will.

"One of the disadvantages of an index strategy is that your growth is restricted. In exchange for protection against market losses, the majority of products that work with an index strategy place a 'cap' on your earnings. I have seen these 'caps' range from 8% to 17%, meaning if the market grows beyond the cap, you will miss out on those gains."

"But we won't *lose* any money, right?" asked Kae.

"That's exactly right. If the market crashes, you won't lose anything. Another disadvantage is that initially, the fees are usually high."

"How high?" asked Will, leaning forward.

"That really depends on how much money you contribute. The fees are typically front-loaded, meaning you pay the majority of them during the first several years of contributions."

"Our mortgage worked like that, right honey?"

"Yes," Will replied, nodding. "For the first ten years or so, the majority of our payments went toward paying the interest of the loan."

"The fees for the products used with index strategies work the same way," said Gene, "and over time, those fees diminish and balance out. In the long-run, the fees really aren't that bad. In some cases (over the life of the policy) the fees average 1-3%, which is very similar to a 401(k) or IRA."

"That doesn't sound bad at all," said Kae.

"Plus, you're saving money on taxes, right?"

Kae and Will both nodded.

"Commissions can also be very, very high, which is unfortunately why most agents sell this product. If you see a policy with a large death benefit, look closer. A large death benefit is typically associated with a high commission.

At Heydari Wealth Group, we are client focused and structure our policies differently. We design our policies with the client in mind because we believe in maximizing our clients' benefits and minimizing our commissions. We invest our own money into indexing strategies and design all of our clients' policies the same way.

"Another disadvantage is that there are surrender charges. If you cancel the policy after a year, the company will charge you a big penalty. They want you to look at this as a long-term strategy, not an overnight get rich quick scheme.

"Well, we're looking for a long-term investment solution, so we shouldn't have any issues with surrender charges," said Will.

"All in all, those disadvantages don't sound too bad," said Kae.

"I don't think so, either. To recap, here are all the pros and cons."

Gene turned his monitor around to face the couple.

Index Strategy	
Pros	Cons
1. Double-Digit Growth Potential 2. Flexibility 3. Protection from Market Crashes 4. Tax-Advantaged Access to Capital & Growth	1. Cap of 11 to 14% 2. Not Accessible in the First Few Contracted Years 3. Higher Initial Costs 4. Surrender Charges

Too Good to Be True?

"OK, how do we get started?" asked Will.

"Before I get into that, I'd like you to keep an open mind. What I'm about to tell you may shock you."

"Now, I'm worried," said Will.

"We've talked, in length, about the power of an index strategy, right?"

The couple nodded.

"So many of us focus on tools, like 401(k)s, brokerage accounts, CDs, etc., when we really should be focusing on the right *strategy*," said Gene.

"I couldn't agree more," said Will.

"Ok, great," replied Gene. "Can we agree that you are looking for strategy that will allow you to take advantage of market volatility, never lose money in market downturns, and grow your money as tax-efficiently as possible, right?"

The Power of the Index

"Yes, definitely," said Will as Kae nodded.

"And I have shown you that an index strategy best accomplishes those goals, right?"

"Right!" exclaimed Kae.

"Well, then the best *tool* for an index strategy is a Wealth Accumulation Engine."

"What's that?" Will asks.

"It's a way for you to grow and accumulate money faster and essentially becomes an engine for your wealth. Once you realize the many advantages it has, this engine can potentially become the foundation of your wealth."

"That sounds incredible. How can we make this happen?" asked Kae.

"We need to do the math and run the numbers, right? I'll gather some information from you today and prepare a personalized retirement blueprint we can review during our next meeting. How does that sound?"

"Sounds like a good plan," said Will.

Gene nodded and smiled. "First, how much money can you set aside each month?"

Kae looked at Will and waited for him to answer.

"I'd say we can afford to put aside about $1,500 a month."

"How old are you?"

"We're both 55," Kae said.

"And when would you like to retire?"

"You tell us!" exclaimed Kae.

"I think what my wife is trying to say is that we'd like to retire as soon as possible."

"But we understand that we may have to work a little longer, dear," she touched her husband's arm, "to make up for those market losses."

Will rolled his eyes and crossed his arms over his chest but nodded.

"How about this? We'll look at a 16-year contribution period. That would retire you at 71. That OK?"

"It's better than I expected, honestly," Will said.

"Well, I can't make any promises, but we'll start there!"

Gene ended the meeting by scheduling a follow-up appointment with Will and Kae. The two were so excited about the strategy, they insisted on coming back the same week. The three settled on Friday.

Gene stood, shook their hands, and watched as his potential new clients walked out the door.

The story continues in the next chapter, but if you're ready to get started <u>now</u>, visit <u>www.TheRetirementEpidemic.com</u> to schedule a free appointment.

Chapter Eleven:

Do You Blindly Follow The Status Quo?

Gene looked at Will and Kae from across his desk. It was Friday and they were still excited about using an index strategy to solve their retirement woes.

"Welcome back. Let's jump right into it, shall we?" said Gene.

"Yes! We can't wait to see what you've put together for us," said Kae.

"That's great to hear," Gene said, laughing.

"To recap, you told me that you can contribute $1,500 a month. You're currently 55, so we decided to contribute to the account for 16 years."

He turned his computer screen around to face the couple.

Age	55
Monthly Contribution	$1,500
Contribution Length	16 Years
Total Contribution Amount	$288,000

"Everything look good?"

Will and Kae nodded.

"Before I show you what an index strategy can do for you, there are a few things to keep in mind."

"I knew there was a catch," said Will.

"No, no catch, just a simple requirement. Earlier this week, we talked about surrender charges. Do you remember?"

They nodded.

"The strategy I'm about to show you will only work correctly as a long-term investment. We recommend keeping the money in the account for at least seven years. If you're looking for something to 'get rich quick', this isn't it."

Will threw his head back and laughed. "We're not looking for that, believe me!"

"Fantastic. Another stipulation I must mention is that the account is regulated by the IRS and there are limits to the amount you can contribute to the account. Just stay within the limits and you'll be fine."

"That shouldn't be a problem, either."

"Will is very good at following the rules!"

"There's nothing stopping us then! Let me show you what an index strategy could do for you.

Tax-Free Cash-Flow

"These numbers are based on a 6% annual return."

"Why 6%?" asked Will.

"Over any 10-year period, our analysis predicts a 92% probability of a 6% return. On average, these accounts see a 7-9% return, but we use 6% because it's conservative."

"Makes sense."

Gene typed into his keyboard and two new rows popped up on his screen.

Age	55
Monthly Contribution	$1,500
Contribution Length	16 Years
Total Contribution Amount	$288,000
Average Return	**6%**
Tax-Free Cash Flow (Age 71-90)	**$55,000**

Will moved to the edge of his seat and leaned toward the screen while Kae searched her purse for her reading glasses.

"Does that say what I think it says?"

"Well, what do you think it says, Will?" said Gene.

"That we'll have $55,000 of tax-free retirement cash flow."

"That's exactly what it says."

"I can't believe it."

"Wait, what?" said Kae. She was still looking for her glasses.

"And we would have that until we turn 90? Is that also right?"

"Yes. That totals $1.1 million in distributions. Plus, if you die before 90, she'll get an added benefit of $275,000, delivered in a lump sum. If you die after 90, she'll get $175,000."

"I really can't believe it," Will said again.

"What if there's an emergency and we have to miss a payment? What happens then?" Kae asked. She had found her glasses and was caught up to speed.

"We always want to put as much money into the policy as possible because we want to take advantage of compounding interest, but the companies that own the contracts are flexible. You can change your payment amounts from year to year, depending on your situation. If you stop funding the account completely, the money will run out of course, but if you take a short break, it's easy to catch-up."

"When the account is structured properly, your money is passed down to your heirs, tax-free."

"Is this new?"

"No, Kae, the strategy isn't new. Wealthy Americans and successful businesses have been using it for over 100 years."

"Why have I never heard of this before?"

"I can't answer that, but maybe it's because Wall street can't make any money off these accounts."

"Oh," she said and sat back in her chair. "That makes a lot of sense."

Can You Keep an Open Mind?

"Before I tell you how to harness the strategy the wealthiest of our country have been using for decades, I'm going to ask you to keep an open mind," said Gene.

"Now, I'm worried," said Will.

"We've talked, in length, about the power of an index strategy, right?"

The couple nodded.

"And I've even shown you how it stands up to the ASERT test."

"Right," said Kae.

"Take another look at this chart."

Strategy	Accessibility	Safety	Expense	Returns	Taxability
IRA	No	no	no	yes	tax deferral
401K	No	no	no	yes	tax deferral
Pension	No	yes	no	yes	tax deferral
CD	Yes	yes	yes	no	taxable
Roth IRA	No	no	no	yes	tax advantage
Stock Market	Yes	no	yes	yes	taxable
Income Properties	No	yes	yes	yes	taxable
Precious Metal	Yes	no	yes	NA	taxable
Hard Money Lending	No	yes	no	yes	taxable
Annuities	No	yes	yes	no	depends
Index Strategy	**Yes**	**yes**	**yes***	**yes**	**tax advantage**

*Initially, life insurance fees are high, but for 15 to 20-year policies, the fees balance out and have a low average cost if funded properly over time.

Will and Kae took their eyes off Gene and once again focused on the screen in front of them.

"By showing you how an index strategy stacks up to the ASERT test, I've also shown you how it compares to other, popular strategies.

"So many of us focus on tools, like 401(k)s, brokerage accounts, CDs, etc., when we really should be focusing on the right *strategy for a portion of your money*," said Gene.

"I couldn't agree more," said Will.

"Ok, great," replied Gene. "Can we also agree that you are looking for strategy that will allow you to take advantage of market volatility, never lose money in market downturns, and grow your money as tax-efficiently as possible, right?"

"Yes, definitely," said Will as Kae nodded.

"And I have shown you that an index strategy best accomplishes those goals, right?"

"Right!" exclaimed Kae.

"Well, then the best *tool* for an index strategy is a Wealth Accumulation Engine Plan wrapped inside a life insurance policy."

What the Wealthy Know That Most Don't

"Did you say life insurance?" Will asked, shaking his head. "I've heard all about life insurance!"

"Will," Kae said, her voice calm, "he asked you to keep an open mind."

Will crossed his arms in front of his chest but didn't say anything else.

"When most people hear 'life insurance' they think about *term* life insurance, or money that is paid out to your heirs after you pass."

Kae nodded.

"But insurance is also an asset category and has been used by some of the world's biggest companies to compensate key executives. Walt Disney, J.C. Penney, and even some U.S. Presidents have used life insurance to grow their wealth," said Gene.

"Really?" asked Kae.

Gene nodded, "Yes. Like I mentioned earlier, the wealthy have been using life insurance as a wealth building and retirement planning vehicle for years. That's why I asked you to keep an open mind. There are some life insurance products out there you should steer clear of, but they aren't *all* bad."

"Then why have I heard so many negative things about life insurance?" asked Will.

"What have you heard?" Gene asked, concerned.

"That it's expensive and agents like you make huge commissions!"

"Yes, if not structured properly, the majority of your premiums will go toward higher costs and higher agent commissions. But, here at the Heydari Wealth Group, we know how to structure the policy to maximize your benefits and minimize our commissions.

"I can see that you're still apprehensive. That's normal! I have to admit, I was skeptical at first, too. But when I realized that life insurance is just a tool that when structured properly, can fully harness the full power of an index strategy, it was hard to ignore.

"Can you see the differences?"

Will squinted his eyes to get a better look at the screen.

Strategy	Accessibility	Safety	Expense	Returns	Taxability
IRA	No	no	no	yes	tax deferral
401K	No	no	no	yes	tax deferral
Pension	No	yes	no	yes	tax deferral
CD	Yes	yes	yes	no	taxable
Roth IRA	No	no	no	yes	tax advantage
Stock Market	Yes	no	yes	yes	taxable
Income Properties	No	yes	yes	yes	taxable
Precious Metal	Yes	no	yes	NA	taxable
Hard Money Lending	No	yes	no	yes	taxable
Annuities	No	yes	yes	no	depends
Wealth Accumulation IUL	Yes	yes	yes*	yes	tax advantage

*Initially, life insurance fees are high, but for 15 to 20-year policies, the fees balance out and have a low average cost.

"Does that say an index strategy gives returns? How does that work again?" asked Will.

"When your money is inside a Wealth Accumulation IUL, it grows with a stock market index, like the S&P 500 or the Dow Jones. When the index sees a positive return, so does your Wealth Accumulation IUL."

"What if the market goes does for ten years in a row? Does that mean I won't see *any* returns?"

"Yes, that's a risk, Will. But keep in mind that the longest losing streak the market has seen was 3 years from 2000 to 2002."

"This really looks great," said Kae. According to this chart, this strategy checks all our boxes."

"I agree," said Gene. "Life insurance, despite its bad reputation, most closely aligns with your Ideal Investment Strategy. It's accessible, inexpensive (over the life of a 20-year policy), delivers returns, and is tax-advantaged."

"I'm surprised," said Will.

"Me, too," replied Kae.

"Like I said, life insurance, built properly, could be a wonderful way to accumulate wealth and become a huge financial engine in your life."

"You keep saying that," said Will.

"Let me explain."

Harness the Full Power of the Index

"First, all the negatives you've heard about life insurance are absolutely true," Gene said with a straight face.

"Come again?" asked Will.

"If you aren't working with the right company, and your policy is built by the wrong agent, it *will* be expensive, and the agent *will* get a huge commission.

"For example, some agents are held captive by the insurance company that employs them. They are required to sell that company's products as-is, regardless of whether or not they'll benefit the client.

"On the other hand, if the agent doesn't know what they're doing, or is looking to make as much money as possible, he or she will structure a traditional policy with a large death benefit. Why? Because the agent's commission is based on the amount of the death benefit.

"There really are eight essential components needed to help ensure the policy performs well. We'll go over those components later, but I want to take a moment to be very clear. If you end up working with an agent who doesn't include these components, there is a good chance your policy won't perform well at all. I hate to say it, but you will probably end up wasting a lot of time and money.

"Here at the Heydari Wealth Group, we know how to harness the full power of an index strategy without charging huge commissions. We are independent and work with insurance companies that allow us to structure policies to benefit our clients first and foremost. We specialize in the types of policies that create a larger amount of wealth accumulation and become a major financial engine in your life. It's all we do!" Gene said, smiling.

"Let's say you want to remodel your kitchen," he said to both Will and Kae. "You want to upgrade your appliances, but you also want new cabinets. Do you hire one professional or two? Do you hire an electrician, a carpenter, or both? I think the answer is obvious...you hire both! An electrician can't do the job of a carpenter or vice versa.

"The same can be said about this type of Wealth Accumulation Plan. There are hundreds of different types of strategies and insurance...so wouldn't you rather work with a company that specializes in designing a Wealth Accumulation Engine Plan for a portion of your money?

"Yes, that makes sense," said Kae.

"Agents with the Heydari Wealth Group aren't going to tell you how to file your taxes because we aren't tax attorneys. We are a team of highly trained Wealth Accumulation Plan specialists and know exactly how to structure policies to harness the power of the index.

"And because Wealth Accumulation IULs are our entire focus, we stay up-to-date and current on all industry changes, meaning we can always recommend the very best companies and options to our clients. The Heydari Wealth Group is different because we ONLY focus on Wealth Accumulation IULs. We are trusted experts."

Will nodded his head slowly.

He had spent most of his life thinking life insurance was a scam, but when he tried to really pinpoint why he thought that, he couldn't. He personally hadn't been burned by life insurance and neither had his or Kae's immediate family...so what was the problem?

Besides, Gene was making a lot of sense. And if the wealthy really had been using the strategy for *years*, maybe it was worth looking in to.

"Ok, you've got me interested," he said, as he grabbed Kae's hand and squeezed. "How are one of these..." He struggled to remember the name. "What do you call them? Wealth Accumulator IULs?"

"Yes," Gene nodded, "that's right."

"How are they structured?"

"Will?" Gene asked, smiling. "I thought you'd never ask. Let me show you exactly how we at the Heydari Wealth Group structure our policies."

How to Structure a Wealth Accumulation IUL

"Take a look at this list," Gene said, and he once again turned his monitor around to face Will and Kae.

The couple stared at the screen.

> **Wealth Accumulation IUL: Account Structure**
> 1. Death Benefit Optimizer
> 2. Cash Max Accelerator
> 3. Expense Reimbursement
> 4. IPA Flex Benefit
> 5. Mutual Insurance
> 6. Market Shadow Crediting
> 7. Loan Options and loan change flexibility
> 8. Critical, Chronic, & Terminal Illness Benefits (not allowed in all states)

"It is critical that your Wealth Accumulation IUL has all of these components, otherwise, your policy may not work to your advantage."

"How will we know if our policy has these components?" asked Will.

"At the Heydari Wealth Group, we structure all our policies to include these eight essential components because like I've mentioned, we use these investment strategies and tools ourselves. We believe our clients should receive all the same benefits we do."

"The structure of the policy sure does sound important," said Kae.

"It is. It's very important your policy contain these eight essential components. Without the right structure, you may end up paying very high fees for a very small return...and waste a lot of time and money in the process."

Chapter Twelve:

How to Grow Your Money Through the Power of Indexed Arbitrage

"Now that I've explained how a Wealth Accumulation IUL is structured, you probably want to know how to use it as a wealth building and retirement planning tool, right?" Gene asked the couple.

"Yes, that would be nice," said Kae, taking a sip of her water.

"Before I do that, we need to be on the same page regarding a basic concept. When it comes to major purchases, do you typically borrow the money or pay in cash?"

"A little bit of both," Will replied. "We typically finance anything more than $25,000 but will use cash to pay for vacations and other electronics, like our phones and laptops."

"That's pretty typical. Have you heard of the bestselling author, R. Nelson Nash?"

Both Will and Kae shook their heads.

"He wrote BANK ON YOURSELF, a book that really fleshes out the concept I'm about to explain. Years ago, he conducted a study on American spending habits and found that on average, most pay 35% of their income on interest charges[55]. That can add up to millions of dollars over a lifetime!"

"I've never thought about it like that," said Will.

"But what if we could do the opposite? Instead of paying all that interest to the bank, what if we could pay that interest to ourselves?"

"Excuse me?" said Kae.

"Can I ask you a question about your car, Kae?" Gene asked.

"Sure," she said. "What do you want to know?"

"Do you own it?"

"We financed it," she said, "and I think we have about 16 more months of payments."

"Do you know your interest rate?"

Kae shook her head and shrugged. She looked at Will.

"Our interest rate is 7% and we bought the car for $25,000."

"What are your monthly payments and how long are the loan terms?" Gene asked.

"Our payments are $495, and we signed a 5-year loan," Will said.

Gene typed the numbers into his computer calculator and turned his monitor around.

> **GOING TO THE BANK**
>
> Borrow $25,000
> 5-year loan (or 60 months)
> 7% Interest
> $495 monthly payment
> Re-pay Total of $29,702
> After 5 years sell car for $12,000
> Lose $4,702 to Interest
> Lose $13,000 to Depreciation
>
> **Total loss $17,702**
>
> **$12,000 to put toward the next car**

"So, you're looking at a repayment amount of $29,702. That's $4,702 or almost 19% in interest."

"What do you mean?" Kae said, her voice high.

He showed them his computer screen.

"When you divide $4,702 by $25,000, the original loan amount, you get 18.8%."

"Oh my..." Kae said and her voice trailed off.

"Mortgages are even worse. At the end of a 30-year fixed mortgage, if they've financed their house once, most people end up paying 100% of the principal in interest. Think about all of that income being wasted on interest rates!"

"That's crazy!" said Kae.

"America's debt really is out of control," Gene continued. "Most of us borrow money to purchase just about everything. Think about all that interest!"

Will shook his head in disbelief. He couldn't help but think about all the interest he and Kae had paid over their lifetimes.

Opportunity Costs

"Do you two know what an opportunity cost is?" Gene asked, snapping Will out of his stupor.

(If you recall, we first introduced "opportunity costs" in Chapter Four.)

"Something about losing money, right?" asked Kae.

"Sort of. When you lose money in the market, for example, you also lose out on the opportunity to invest that money (and make gains) elsewhere. When you finance something and pay interest, you give up your opportunity to make money on that money.

"For example, we just determined that you're spending about $4,700 in interest on your car, right?"

Will and Kae both nodded.

"If you didn't have to pay that money in interest, you could invest it, meaning your opportunity cost isn't just the $4,700 in interest, it's all the money that $4,700 could earn in your lifetime. As you can imagine, if you add up all the interest you've paid over your lifetime, *and* calculate the opportunity costs associated with that interest, the amount really can be quite staggering."

"So, we should be paying cash?" asked Will, his nose crinkled in confusion.

"Paying cash is just as bad because it's a guaranteed loss. When you buy something in cash, that cash is no longer earning interest for you, right? When you pay in cash, you give up future earnings on that cash."

"Now I'm really confused," said Kae, rubbing her eyes with the palms of her hands. "Financing is bad, but paying in cash is bad, too, right?"

"It can be," replied Gene.

"Ok...but how are we supposed to pay for things?"

Borrow from Yourself

"There IS a third option," Gene said. "It's what corporations and the wealthiest in our country do."

"Ok," said Kae, "so what is it?"

"You can borrow from yourself."

Will and Kae looked at Gene from across the desk. They were clearly confused.

"This ties back to using life insurance to grow your wealth and fund your retirement. When structured properly, a life insurance tool can be used as a cash storage device. You can access that money for major purchases, like cars and houses, by borrowing against it. That's what makes the strategy accessible."

"How is that different from saving?" asked Kae.

"I'm glad you asked! This is the most exciting component to life insurance! Unlike your savings account, the cash value inside your life insurance policy never stops earning interest. When you borrow from your cash value, the life insurance company that manages the policy uses your policy as collateral.

"It works the same way with a mortgage, right? When you borrow from the bank, you agree to pay that loan back within a certain amount of time. If you miss too many payments, they will foreclose on that house. They hold the house as collateral. All the while, the house (in most cases) continues to appreciate in value. Over time, the house *should* be worth more.

"The cash value inside your life insurance policy works just like that. It continues to appreciate in value, regardless of any loans made against it," Gene said, smiling. He loved talking about the power of life insurance!

"That's pretty unbelievable," said Will, shaking his head.

"I had a hard time believing it at first, too," said Gene, "but like I said, most businesses and the majority of America's wealthy have been doing it for years! It's how they avoid paying interest charges! They borrow from themselves, and then pay themselves back."

"Wow," said Kae as her jaw dropped.

"I've used this strategy personally. Just recently, I borrowed against my policy to buy myself a new car. I use it for all of my big purchases because I continue to earn interest on the money I borrow."

Tax-Free Benefits Galore

"And, it gets even better. Remember when I told you an index strategy is tax efficient?"

Will and Kae nodded.

"It's tax-efficient in two ways. First, because we're taking a *loan* against the cash value inside our life insurance policy, we don't have to pay taxes."

"You don't?" asked Kae.

"Have you ever had to pay taxes on a loan? For example, when you borrowed the $25,000 for your car, Kae, did you have to pay taxes on that loan?"

"No, of course not," she said.

"You don't have to pay taxes on money you borrow from a life insurance policy, either. This is what makes it a tax-efficient retirement planning tool. You can 'borrow' against your policy in retirement and access your cash tax-free."

"That is really something!" Will said as he slapped the top of this thigh.

"It really is," said Gene, smiling. "You can also pass the policy down to your heirs, tax-free."

"Now I know you're pulling my leg," said Will.

"It's all written in the Internal Revenue Code, subsection 7702. Money inside life insurance policies, if specific guidelines are met, can be passed down to your heirs tax-free[56]."

He turned his computer monitor around to face the couple.

Section 72(e) and 7702

The most unique feature of permanent life insurances is that under Section 72(e) and 7702 of the Internal Revenue Code the accumulation of cash inside the insurance contract is tax advantaged. Not only can the cash value accumulate tax-free, but the cash can also be accessed tax-free.

Hence, the living benefit of life insurance: It is a unique vehicle that allows tax-free account value accumulation, allows you to access your money tax-free, and, when you die, blossoms in the value and transfers income tax-free!

"Let's say you decide to use a Wealth Accumulation IUL to save for your retirement. There is a death benefit attached to your policy, meaning when you pass away, your beneficiary will get the death benefit tax-free."

A Tool Everyone Should Use

"This is incredibly exciting!" exclaimed Kae.

"Yes, yes, it is," said Will, smiling. For the first time since he learned the news of his botched 401(k) retirement plan, he felt good, like there was some hope.

"Great! I'm glad you're excited about it. During our next meeting, we can discuss the ins and outs, and how to get started. We can also take a hard look at your accounts and devise a plan of attack. How does that sound?"

"We can't get started now?" asked Kae.

"I would like you to do some research, first. Before you leave, I'll give you some material to read. It should only take about 10-15 minutes."

"Ok, great," said Will.

"Also, just something to think about, because using an index strategy requires partnering with a life insurance company, you will have to qualify."

"Qualify?" asked Kae.

"Yes. Because there are underwriters involved, you will likely need to get a physical. But we can talk more about that during our next meeting. The packet I give you should answer most of your questions."

"Overall, a Wealth Accumulation IUL will provide you with a solid financial foundation and peace of mind. You won't have to worry about the market dropping. You also won't have to worry about emergencies. If you need to access your money, there are no age restrictions; you can get it at any time."

"It just keeps getting better. Thank you for your time, Gene," Will said as he stood and shook the agent's hand.

"It was my pleasure! I think life insurance is a tool that everyone should be using to plan for retirement and grow wealth. Like we've talked about, the benefits are huge! An index strategy really does check all those 'perfect investment strategy' boxes. It's accessible, inexpensive (over the life of the policy), and tax-efficient."

Gene shook Kae's hand next and handed Will a pamphlet of information on how to build a Wealth Accumulation plan.

The couple, smiling, walked hand in hand out the door.

Are you ready to follow in Will and Kae's footsteps? There is never a better time to start than right now. Visit www.TheRetirementEpidemic.com to schedule a complimentary appointment.

Chapter Thirteen:
Leveraged Wealth Arbitrage

I could probably write an entire 200-page book on this topic, but for now, I will simply give you a brief overview of how powerful this strategy can be.

If you think a Wealth Accumulation IUL account is powerful, just wait until you learn about Leveraged Wealth Arbitrage (LWA).

But before I continue, I must warn you: this chapter is exclusively designed for investors with a net worth of at least $3 million.

LWA is like a Wealth Accumulation Plan on steroids; it harnesses the massive power of leverage.

Successful investors and business owners understand the power of leverage. It's something the wealthy have been using to grow their wealth for decades.

What is leverage?

In finance, it refers to "an investment strategy using borrowed money[57]". In my industry specifically, when used correctly, has the power to potentially quadruple your return...in half the time of a Wealth Accumulation Plan.

Before I explain how an LWA works, first let's take a look at why you should consider this strategy:

Leveraged Wealth Arbitrage - Advantages

1. You don't need to liquidate other good-performing assets and pay penalties and taxes
2. You can leverage someone else's money to grow your own money
3. You can take advantage of the current low-interest rate environment
4. It quantitatively outperforms a managed investment account
5. It thrives in the heaviest stress-test simulation in the industry
6. You get even more protection for your family and business at a fraction of the cost
7. You can potentially deduct interest payments
8. It provides you with tax-free cash flow in retirement

How to Maximize Your ROI

When it comes to funding your plan, there are a few options.

Option #1: Fund the Plan Monthly or Annually

This option is pretty straightforward.

Option #2: Frontload the Account

This simply means to invest more (sometimes a lot more) over the first 3-7 years you own the policy. This is beneficial because when you frontload the account, the power of compounding interest works to your advantage faster. Think about it. You have a larger account balance at the beginning, meaning that balance has a lot longer to grow.

Option #2 sounds great, right? The problem is that many people simply don't have the ability to deposit $1 million into an indexed account in one lump sum (or $200 thousand each year for five years, for that matter). And for many, liquidating well-preforming assets to front-load an index account might not make sense.

Option #3: Leveraged Wealth Arbitrage*

This unique program was originally developed for clients with a net worth of $25 million or more because the majority of this demographic (business owners) understand the power of leverage and positive interest arbitrage.

When we create a Leveraged Wealth Arbitrage Account (LWAA), we arrange for a lender to frontload the indexed account. In subsequent years, the client pays interest-only payments to the lender, leveraging the lender's ability to infuse a larger amount into the indexed account on behalf of the client. Essentially, we leverage Other People's Money (OPM) and make it work to the benefit of our clients.

Simple vs. Compound Interest

Let me explain how it works.

Say you want to fund your Wealth Accumulation IUL with a $400,000 premium for the next 20 years, that means you're contributing approximately $20,000 dollars annually.

For most of us, that's a very affordable payment... but, that affordability means the account grows slowly.

Conceptually, a LWAA is the same as a Wealth Accumulation IUL, but it grows much, much faster.

Instead of funding the account for 20 years, you fund it for four years at $100,000 a year. Then you let it sit and earn interest for the remaining 16 investment years.

But the biggest difference is that instead of funding the policy yourself, you borrow it from the bank.

Why is this important?

The sooner we can get that $400,000 in our LWAA earning interest, the better, right? By borrowing the money from the bank, you can do just that, all without liquidating your assets.

You might be thinking...

But if I have to pay interest to the bank, what's the point?

The difference is purely mathematical.

> We then leverage the bank's money to fund the policy. We pay **simple interest** on the money we owe the bank, and we earn **compounded interest** on the money we have invested.

It works just like a mortgage.

When you borrow money from the bank to buy a house, you are paying the bank simple interest while the house appreciates (hopefully) in value.

Leveraged Wealth Arbitrage works the same way. You earn more in compound interest than you owe the bank in simple interest.

Let's take a look at an example:

Wealth Advantaged Account		Leveraged Wealth Arbitrage		
Year	Premium	Front load premiums		
1	50,000	150,000	4.00%	6,000
2	50,000	150,000	4.00%	12,000
3	50,000	150,000	4.00%	18,000
4	50,000	150,000	4.00%	24,000
5	50,000	150,000	4.00%	30,000
6	50,000		4.00%	30,000
7	50,000		4.00%	30,000
8	50,000		4.00%	30,000
9	50,000		4.00%	30,000
10	50,000		4.00%	30,000
11	50,000		4.00%	30,000
12	50,000		4.00%	30,000
13	50,000		4.00%	30,000
14	50,000		4.00%	30,000
15	50,000		4.00%	30,000
	750,000			390,000
Tax Free Cash Flow				
16	85,000			140,000
50	85,000			140,000
	2,975,000			4,900,000

What About High-Interest Rate Environments?

When applied properly, a LWAA is how you can grow your wealth the fastest.

Let me give you an example to demonstrate the power of a Leveraged Wealth Arbitrage Account.

If your account is funded with $2 million of cumulative borrowed premiums and the borrowing rate is 4%, the annual simple interest payment to the lender is $80,000.

To drive my point home, let's say the LWAA's account grows at the same rate, at 4%. In 20 years, the account will grow to $4,382,246. In the 21st year, again assuming a meager 4% gain, the account will see a $175,290 annual increase.

That's quite a bit more than the $80,000 we owe the bank in interest, right?

For some of you, this concept isn't new. You've heard all about premium financing and think it only works when interest rates at the bank are low.

That is a valid concern, but it simply isn't the case. Seeing growth in an LWAA with a high-interest rate environment is still possible.

Even if the interest we owe the bank increases to 7% and our account return remains at 4%, *we still make money.*

An increase to 7% means an increased interest payment of $140,000 annually, and a negative interest arbitrage of -3%. But the power of compound interest still **produces a $25,290 *positive* dollar arbitrage.**

> ### Why Should Banks Loan You the Money?
>
> You might be asking...
>
> "Why would banks ever lend out money for a Leveraged Wealth Arbitrage Account?"
>
> This is another misconception. Banks *want* to loan you the money.
>
> That is because the loan is collateralized, backed up by both the account's death benefit and cash value. Banks love making these types of loans because they're 100% foolproof (in most cases).
>
> And if you're questioning the legitimacy of the insurance company managing the LWAA, don't. The insurance companies my firm works with are all A+ Rated, and in their 300-year history, have never missed a death benefit payout.
>
> Like I said, the bank is guaranteed to make their money back. The question you really should be asking yourself is...
>
> "Why *shouldn't* the bank loan me money?"

The Power of Leveraged Wealth Arbitrage

The power of premium financing and a Leveraged Wealth Arbitrage Account has only been made available for those Americans with $25 million or more in cash net worth...until now.

Today, through our unique banking and lending partnerships, we have produced an exclusive program available to those of you with varying levels of net worth. I am a part of a very specific group of investors and financial planners who have been able to put a program together for people with $3 to $10 million of net worth.

Our slogan is "Do the Math," because the results our clients experience are indisputable.

We don't speculate, guess, or theorize...

We don't use a crystal ball...

What we demonstrate is the undeniable mathematical outcome our program offers.

How do we do that?

We compare it to any other investment alternative in any historical "lookback" period of time. Once you see the irrefutable mathematical outcome our program produces, you will not only become a client, you'll also become a huge fan.

The Underlying Investment and How It Works

So, how do we do it? How do we take your wealth to the next level?

It's all in the magic of how we structure the account.

Like a Wealth Accumulation IUL, the **Underlying Investment** in the LWA program is an index fund that is correlated with the S&P 500.

The index is credited using a 0% floor and a 5-Point Market Shadow. This means that if the S&P 500 produces a negative return, you won't lose any of your gains or principal balance. The 5-Point Market Shadow means that your index account earns five points less than whatever the S&P 500 produces.

Meaning, if the S&P 500 produces a -38.49% return like it did in 2008, your index account will lose 0%. If the S&P 500 produces a +29.43% return like it did in 2013, your index account will be credited +24.43% (5.00% less than the gross return[58]).

Year	Index Gross Returns	Policy Credit
1999	26.67%	21.67%
2000	19.53%	14.53%
2001	-10.14%	0.00%
2002	-13.04%	0.00%
2003	-23.37%	0.00%
2004	26.38%	21.38%
2005	8.99%	3.99%
2006	3.00%	0.00%

2007	13.60%	8.60%
2008	3.52%	0.00%
2009	-38.49%	0.00%
2010	23.65%	18.65%
2011	12.63%	7.63%
2012	0.10%	0.00%
2013	13.29%	8.29%
2014	29.43%	24.43%
2015	11.54%	6.54%
2016	-0.73%	0.00%
2017	9.54%	4.54%
2018	19.42%	14.42%

Please note: The 5% shadow used in the example above is subject to change.

Our second focus is on the product used to house the investment. We use a Leveraged Arbitrage Wealth Account, an index account wrapped inside a life insurance policy.

We use a life insurance policy for three reasons:
1. The gains are tax-deferred
2. Those gains can be accessed tax-free and without early-withdrawal penalties
3. We can pass our death benefit onto our beneficiaries tax-free

We don't believe in smoke and mirror tricks because we don't have to. An LWAA is *that* powerful.

Exclusive Lending Parameters

We have unique relationships with lenders and banking institutions that allow us to uniquely design Leveraged Wealth Arbitrage Accounts.

Our partnerships and exclusive lending parameters allow us to offer no personal guarantor and no additional collateral requirements.

In addition, the loan isn't reported to the credit bureaus, meaning it has no effect on your personal credit score or **DTI (Debt-To-Income)** ratio. If the policy is corporate-owned, it has no effect on the company's balance sheet.

Also, because the account is managed through a life insurance policy, the loan is a **nonrecourse debt**, secured by that collateral we talked about (the policy's cash value and death benefit).

Finally, we can create these accounts very, very quickly. Underwriting the loan can be executed in two to three weeks.

Historical Math Doesn't Lie

The way we structure and design our Leveraged Wealth Arbitrage Accounts is powerful...but our 10- to 40-year look back may be the most valuable service we provide for our clients.

We can back-test our program over the last 10, 20, 30, and 40 years to compare the performances of both an LWAA account and a traditionally managed investment account. We break this test into four categories.

1. 40-Year Look-Back:

This model is pretty straight forward, simply the last 40 years of the S&P 500.

2. 20-Year Look-Back:

We created a hypothetical 40-year period by taking the last 20 years and ran this 20-year period back-to-back, creating a hypothetical 40-year period.

3. The Best 20-Year Period:

We created another hypothetical 40-year period by taking the best 20-year period of the S&P 500 (1980-1999) and running this 20-year period back-to-back, thus creating another hypothetical 40-year period. During this period of time the CAGR of the S&P 500 was 17.99%.

4. The Sandwich Period:

We created another hypothetical 40-year period by using the worst 10-year period of the S&P 500 for the first 10 years, (2000-2009) then using the last 20-year period for years 11-30, then using the worst 10-year period again for years 31-40.

When we analyzed these four categories, we found that in each one of those cases, the Leveraged Wealth Arbitrage Account produced a substantially greater return than mutual funds, managed investment accounts, and qualified retirement plans.

> Our Leveraged Wealth Arbitraged Account offers three key elements: no interest accrual, no high-cash value rider, and no over-leveraged policy design.

What Makes LWA Different?

Traditional Premium Financing comes with a lot of risks:

1. Possible negative interest arbitrage from poor policy performance
2. Increased borrowing rates
3. Additional collateral calls

These challenges typically stem from overleveraging the policy which typically means a policy design and poor lending restrictions.

We want the cash value in the policy to be more than the net value of the loan. Policies that are structured poorly will give you just the opposite.

Advantages and Disadvantages

Like with every investment, Leveraged Wealth Arbitrage Accounts have both advantages and *disadvantages*. As exciting as these accounts are, they also have some built in risk. These accounts aren't right for everyone.

But if you strongly believe an LWAA is right for you and are serious about building your wealth quickly, contact me to see if you qualify. Visit www.TheRetirementEpidemic.com to schedule a complimentary consultation.

Leveraged Wealth Arbitrage Account	
Advantages	Disadvantages
You don't need to liquidate assets, pay penalties or taxes because you use the bank's money to fund the account	If the interest rate goes up, you may need to post additional collateral
You can take advantage of low interest rates to maximize positive arbitrage	The policy may not perform well if the market sees multiple down years
An LWAA outperforms most managed investment accounts	
An increased death benefit (business or personal)	
Potential interest payment deductions	

Curing the Retirement Epidemic

At the very beginning of this book, I claimed there was a cancer infecting America...a disease out to contaminate the way our country retires.

I showed you how the market, taxes, interest rates and inflation can all exasperate and help spread the Retirement Epidemic and leave you either broke or penniless.

But in spite of all that doom and gloom, there is hope. We are fortunate to live in a financial time that offers us many unique and powerful solutions.

For most of us, a Wealth Accumulation IUL, when used correctly, can not only help solve our problems and provide income in retirement, but help generate true wealth as well.

And for those of you who earn $3 million or more and are serious about quadrupling your wealth in half the time, there are elite options for you, too. A Leveraged Wealth Arbitrage Accounts is a powerful wealth-building tool, and one that is now accessible to you.

So, what are you waiting for?

Now, is the time for action! Now, is the time to start protecting and *growing* your wealth exponentially.

Cure the Retirement Epidemic and unlock your true wealth potential. Visit www.TheRetirementEpidemic.com to schedule your complimentary consultation today!

CALL TO ACTION

There's a disease spreading across America. It's been growing and festering for decades, threatening to infect the financial futures of millions of Americans.

I'm talking about America's Retirement Income Crisis, a plague aimed to ruin the hopes and dreams of retirees across the country.

Is there a retirement income crisis?

I believe, wholeheartedly, that there is. People aren't saving enough for retirement. It's an epidemic.

<u>More than half of Americans between the ages of 56 and 61 have less than $17,000 saved for retirement</u>...

Can you believe that?

Now, think about your own retirement savings... where do you stack up?

The Retirement Income Crisis is a cancerous epidemic that is infecting generations of retirees.

Too many of us are relying on social security, losing millions to market losses, opportunity costs, and taxes. We are also vastly overestimating the fortitude of our nest eggs.

Regardless of the reason, the spread of this infectious disease must be stopped.

The good news is that there is hope. There is a light at the end of this dark, cancer-ridden retirement tunnel.

Over the 9+ years I've been in business, through trial and error, I have discovered little known strategies that can help boost your savings and generate additional income, all without having to change your lifestyle.

With the right strategy and the right tools, I can help grow your wealth, cancer-free. Visit www.TheRetirementEpidemic.com to schedule a complimentary consultation.

ACKNOWLEDGEMENTS:

I never thought I would be writing a book about something that I'm so passionate about.

I hope this book reaches as many people as possible and shows them an alternative way to grow their money, outside of Wall Street, and how to become financially independent.

First and foremost, I would like to thank my parents who raised me right, and who supported me emotionally and financially. They taught me that with dedication, hard work, and perseverance, anything can be done.

When it seemed too difficult to complete this book, thank you to all my friends for all the encouragement. Thank you for listening, offering me advice, and supporting me throughout this entire process.

I would also like to thank my mentor, Ethan Kap, for his guidance and thoughtful insights.

And lastly, I would like to thank my editor who helped me edit, proofread, and organize my thoughts.

End Notes

1. Monique Morrissey, "The State of American Retirement" *Economic Policy Institute*, March 3, 2016 http://www.epi.org/publication/retirement-in-america/#charts (accessed July 22, 2018).
2. "Life expectancy in the USA, 1990-98, men and women" *University of California at Berkeley* http://www.demog.berkeley.edu/~andrew/1918/figure2.html (accessed July 22, 2018).
3. "United States Selected Rankings" *Geoba.se*, http://www.geoba.se/country.php?cc=US&year=2018 (accessed July 22, 2018).
4. Thomsen Prentice, "Health, history and hard choices: Funding dilemmas in a fast-changing world" *World Health Organization*, August, 2006 http://www.who.int/global_health_histories/seminars/presentation07.pdf (accessed July 22, 2018).
5. "Survey of Consumer Sciences" *Board of Governors of the Federal Reserve System* https://www.federalreserve.gov/econres/aboutscf.htm (accessed July 22, 2018).

6. Alicia H. Munnell, Anthony Webb, and Francesca Golub-Sass, "The National Retirement Risk Index: An Update" *Center for Retirement Research at Boston College*, October 2012 http://crr.bc.edu/wp-content/uploads/2012/11/IB_12-20-508.pdf (accessed July 22, 2018).

7. Justin McCarthy, "Americans' Financial Anxieties Ease in 2017" *Gallup,* May 19, 2017 http://news.gallup.com/poll/210890/americans-financial-anxieties-ease-2017.aspx (accessed July 22, 2018).

8. Lea Hart, "Americans' biggest retirement fear: Running out of Money" *Journal of Accountancy,* October 6, 2016 https://www.journalofaccountancy.com/news/2016/oct/americans-fear-running-out-of-retirement-money-201615242.html (accessed July 22, 2018).

9. "Ultimate guide to retirement" *CNN Money* http://money.cnn.com/retirement/guide/SocialSecurity_basics.moneymag/index.htm (accessed July 22, 2018).

10. Selena Maranjian, "Americans' Average Social Security at Age 62, 66, and 70" *The Motley Fool*, July 30, 2017 https://www.fool.com/retirement/2017/07/30/americans-average-social-security-at-age-62-66-and.aspx (accessed July 22, 2018).

11. Lindsay Wissman, "2017 Federal Poverty Level Guidelines" *PeopleKeep*, February 7, 2017 https://www.zanebenefits.com/blog/2017-federal-poverty-level-guidelines (accessed July 22, 2018).

12. Denver Nowicz, "Your 5 best arguments for life insurance besides the death benefit" *Wealth For Life* http://wealthforlife.net/your-5-best-arguments-for-life-insurance-besides-the-death-benefit/ (accessed July 22, 2018).

13. "History of taxation in the United States" *Wikipedia* https://en.wikipedia.org/wiki/Taxation_history_of_the_United_States (accessed July 22, 2018).

14. Erin El Issa, "2017 American Household Credit Card Debt Study" *NerdWallet* https://www.nerdwallet.com/blog/

End Notes

average-credit-card-debt-household/ (accessed July 22, 2018).

15. "Revenue Act of 1978" *Wikipedia* https://en.wikipedia.org/wiki/Revenue_Act_of_1978 (accessed July 22, 2018).

16. Scott Tong, "Father of modern 401(k) says it fails many Americans" *MarketPlace*, June 13, 2013 https://www.marketplace.org/2013/06/13/sustainability/consumed/father-modern-401k-says-it-fails-many-americans (accessed July 22, 2018).

17. "History of 401(k)s Plans: An Update" *Employee Benefit Research Institute*, February 2005 https://www.ebri.org/pdf/publications/facts/0205fact.a.pdf (accessed July 22, 2018).

18. "Life expectancy in the USA, 1990-98, men and women" *University of California at Berkeley* http://www.demog.berkeley.edu/~andrew/1918/figure2.html (accessed July 22, 2018).

19. "Average life expectancy in North America for those born in 2017, by gender and region (in years)" *Statista* https://www.statista.com/statistics/274513/life-expectancy-in-north-america/ (accessed July 22, 2018).

20. Gayle L. Reznik, Dave Shoffner, and David A. Weaver, "Coping with the Demographic Challenge: Fewer Children and Living Longer" *Social Security Office of Policy* https://www.ssa.gov/policy/docs/ssb/v66n4/v66n4p37.html) (accessed July 22, 2018).

21. Stephen C. Goss, "The Future Financial Status of the Social Security Program" *Social Security Office of Retirement and Disability Policy* https://www.ssa.gov/policy/docs/ssb/v70n3/v70n3p111.html#mn1 (accessed July 22, 2018).

22. Andrew Beattie, "Market Crashes: The Great Depression (1929)" *Investopedia* https://www.investopedia.com/features/crashes/crashes5.asp (accessed July 22, 2018).

23. "Bank run" *Wikipedia* https://en.wikipedia.org/wiki/Bank_run (accessed July 22, 2018).

24. "11 historic bear markets" *NBC News* http://www.nbcnews.com/id/37740147/ns/business-stocks_and_economy/t/historic-bear-markets/#.Wmi8K66nFaQ (accessed July 22, 2018).

25. "A Detailed Analysis of U.S. Bear Markets" *Moon Capital Management* March, 2016 http://www.mooncap.com/wp-content/uploads/2016/04/bear-markets-Mar2016.pdf (accessed July 22, 2018).

26. "Opinion: Americans are still terrible at investing, annual study once again shows" *MarketWatch*, October 21, 2017 https://www.marketwatch.com/story/americans-are-still-terrible-at-investing-annual-study-once-again-shows-2017-10-19 (accessed July 22, 2018).

27. "A Detailed Analysis of U.S. Bear Markets" *Moon Capital Management* March, 2016 http://www.mooncap.com/wp-content/uploads/2016/04/bear-markets-Mar2016.pdf (accessed July 22, 2018).

28. "Warren Buffett Quotes" *BrainyQuote* https://www.brainyquote.com/quotes/warren_buffett_149683 (accessed July 22, 2018).

29. "Dalbar's 22nd Annual Quantitative Analysis of Investor Behavior, For period ended: 12.31.2015" *Dalbar* https://www.qidllc.com/wp-content/uploads/2016/02/2016-Dalbar-QAIB-Report.pdf (accessed July 22, 2018).

30. David M. Walker, "Commentary: Why your taxes could double" *CNN Politics,* April 15, 2009 http://www.cnn.com/2009/POLITICS/04/15/walker.tax.debt/index.html (accessed July 22, 2018).

31. "How CBO Produces Fair-Value Estimates of the Cost of Federal Credit Programs: A Primer" *Congressional Budget Office* (p 8), July 2018 https://www.cbo.gov/system/files?file=2018-07/53886-FairValuePrimer.pdf (accessed July 22, 2018).

32. "Eight Charts that Show the Growth in Government" *The Budget Book: 106 Ways to Reduce the Size & Scope of*

End Notes

Government https://budgetbook.heritage.org/eight-charts-show-growth-government/ (accessed July 22, 2018).

33. Kimberly Amadeo, "Debt-to GDP Ratio, Its Formula, and How to Use It" *The Balance*, July 15, 2018 https://www.thebalance.com/debt-to-gdp-ratio-how-to-calculate-and-use-it-3305832 (accessed July 22, 2018).

34. D.H. Taylor, "The Big Mac Index May Be Telling The Truth About Inflation" *SeekingAlpha*, November 1, 2017 https://seekingalpha.com/article/4119246-big-mac-index-may-telling-truth-inflation (accessed July 22, 2018).

35. David John Marotta, "Big Mac Index Shows Official CPI Underreports Inflation" *Forbes*, April 16, 2013 https://www.forbes.com/sites/davidmarotta/2013/04/16/big-mac-index-shows-official-cpi-underreports-inflation/#1ad8ba9c3551 (accessed July 22, 2018).

36. "Inflation" *Dictionary.com* http://www.dictionary.com/browse/inflation?s=t (accessed July 22, 2018).

37. Tim Wilhoit, "Accumulate Wealth with the Rule of 72" *LinkedIn*, June 5, 2014 https://www.linkedin.com/pulse/20140605133849-94293277-accumulate-wealth-with-the-rule-of-72/ (accessed July 22, 2018).

38. "Rule of 72" *Investopedia* https://www.investopedia.com/terms/r/ruleof72.asp (accessed July 22, 2018).

39. "The Typical American's Problem" *Infinite Banking* http://www.infinitebanking.org/wp-content/uploads/2012/12/Lecture-1-Notes.pdf (accessed July 22, 2018).

40. Erin El Issa, "2017 American Household Credit Card Debt Study" *NerdWallet* https://www.nerdwallet.com/blog/average-credit-card-debt-household/ (accessed July 22, 2018).

41. "The average U.S. household debt continues to rise" *Credit Karma*, December 15, 2017 https://www.creditkarma.com/studies/i/average-debt-american-household-on-rise/ (accessed July 22, 2018).

42. "Four Percent Rule" *Investopedia* https://www.investopedia.com/terms/f/four-percent-rule.asp (accessed July 22, 2018).
43. "Gold Rush (TV series)" *Wikipedia* https://en.wikipedia.org/wiki/Gold_Rush_(TV_series) (accessed July 22, 2018).
44. "Placer mining" *Wikipedia* https://en.wikipedia.org/wiki/Placer_mining (accessed July 22, 2018).
45. "Gold Rush (TV series)" *Wikipedia* https://en.wikipedia.org/wiki/Gold_Rush_(TV_series) (accessed July 22, 2018).
46. Brad E.S. Tinnon,"Beware of Gold Commercials" *Best Wealth Management,* December 1, 2016 https://bestwealth.net/beware-gold-commercials/ (accessed July 22, 2018).
47. "Gold Prices – 100 Year Historical Chart" *MacroTrends* http://www.macrotrends.net/1333/historical-gold-prices-100-year-chart (accessed July 22, 2018).
48. "Executive Order 6102" *Wikipedia* https://en.wikipedia.org/wiki/Executive_Order_6102 (accessed July 22, 2018).
49. "Bridge to Nowhere" *Wikipedia* https://en.wikipedia.org/wiki/Bridge_to_Nowhere_(San_Gabriel_Mountains) (accessed August 1, 2018).
50. "Table 1300. Age of reference person: Annual expenditure means, shares, standard errors, and coefficients of variation, Consumer Expenditure Survey, 2016" U.S. *Bureau of Labor Statistics* https://www.bls.gov/cex/2016/combined/age.pdf (accessed August 1, 2018).
51. "Los Angeles flood of 1938" *Wikipedia* https://en.wikipedia.org/wiki/Los_Angeles_flood_of_1938 (accessed August 1, 2018).
52. "Table 1300. Age of reference person: Annual expenditure means, shares, standard errors, and coefficients of variation, Consumer Expenditure Survey, 2016" U.S. *Bureau of Labor Statistics* https://www.bls.gov/cex/2016/combined/age.pdf (accessed August 1, 2018).
53. "Historical Background and Development of Social Security" *Social Security* https://www.ssa.gov/history/briefhistory3.html (accessed August 1, 2018).

End Notes

54. "Life expectancy in the USA, 1900-98" *University of California at Berkeley* http://www.demog.berkeley.edu/~andrew/1918/figure2.html (accessed August 1, 2018).

55. "Average* life expectancy in North America for those born in 2017, by gender and region (in years)" *Statista* https://www.statista.com/statistics/274513/life-expectancy-in-north-america/ (accessed August 1, 2018).

56. "The Typical American's Problem" *Infinite Banking* http://www.infinitebanking.org/wp-content/uploads/2012/12/Lecture-1-Notes.pdf (accessed July 22, 2018).

57. "Application of Sections 7702 and 7702A to Life Insurance Contracts that Mature After Age 100" *Internal Revenue Service* https://www.irs.gov/pub/irs-drop/n-09-47.pdf (accessed July 22, 2018).

58. "Leverage" *Investopedia* https://www.investopedia.com/terms/l/leverage.asp (accessed July 22, 2018).

59. "Leveraged Index Arbitrage" *Lionsmark Capital* http://www.lionsmarkcapital.com/Lionsmark/LIONSMARK_CAPITAL.html (accessed July 22, 2018).